Brilliant e-Citizen

PEARSON EDUCATION HIGHER EDUCATION DIVISION

We work with leading authors to develop the strongest
educational materials in computing, bringing cutting-edge
thinking and best learning practice to a global market.

Under a range of well-known imprints, including Pearson
Prentice Hall, we craft high quality print and electronic
publications which help readers to understand and apply
their content, whether studying or at work.

To find out more about the complete range of our
publishing, please visit us on the World Wide Web at:
www.pearsoned.co.uk

Brilliant e-Citizen

Nik Taylor

PEARSON
Prentice
Hall

Harlow, England • London • New York • Boston • San Francisco • Toronto • Sydney • Singapore • Hong Kong
Tokyo • Seoul • Taipei • New Delhi • Cape Town • Madrid • Mexico City • Amsterdam • Munich • Paris • Milan

Pearson Education Limited
Edinburgh Gate
Harlow
Essex CM20 2JE
England

and Associated Companies throughout the world

Visit us on the World Wide Web at:
www.pearsoned.co.uk

First published 2007

ISBN-13: 978-0-13-174394-6
ISBN-10: 0-13-174394-5

British Library Cataloguing-in-Publication Data
A catalogue record for this book is available from the British Library

Library of Congress Cataloging-in-Publication Data
A catalog record for this book is available from the Library of Congress

10 9 8 7 6 5 4 3 2 1
10 09 08 07

Typeset in Helvetica Roman 9pt on 12pt by 30
Printed and bound by Ashford Colour Press, Gosport

The publisher's policy is to use paper manufactured from sustainable forests.

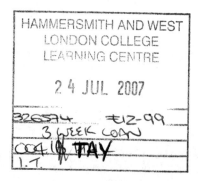

Contents

CHAPTER 1

Getting Started with Computers

1.1 Introduction

Welcome! Since you've picked up this book, chances are you want to improve your skills at using a computer. Good call. As you've probably noticed, computers are everywhere these days, and knowing how to use one can open up stacks of possibilities to you.

For instance, you'll be able to use simple software programs to create professional-looking documents, or easily make complex calculations. You'll be able to get in touch with friends and family via email, even if they live half the world away. You can go shopping without leaving your seat, book travel tickets or read the latest news headlines by simply opening a web browser. The e-Citizen qualification exists to enable you to learn enough about computers to accomplish all these tasks and more. Working your way through this book will teach you all the skills you need to pass the e-Citizen exam.

In this first chapter, you'll start at the very beginning. That means learning to do basic tasks, such as turning on your computer, and understanding the names of all the main parts of your system. Once you've got the PC 'booted up' (geek speak for turning it on!), you'll then need to go through the process of logging on, so your computer knows who's talking to it.

With that done, you're ready to start giving your computer instructions. This is done either by using the mouse, or by typing in using your keyboard. The mouse in particular can seem a daunting piece of technology to anyone who's not used a computer before – but it really doesn't take long to get to grips with it. Once you know how to use a mouse, you can speed up your time on the computer using double clicks, right clicks and more.

The keyboard, on the other hand, will look familiar to anyone who's ever used a typewriter. However, there's a lot more to be found on a computer keyboard, and with a little know-how you can use the extra keys to make your work on the PC much, much easier.

Once you're finished with your computer session, it's important you go through the correct procedure to shut it down. If you don't, you run the risk of having something go wrong with your PC later on.

Confused by computing lingo?

You should find that this book explains all you need to know in easy-to-understand, non-technical language. However, if you come across any puzzling computing terms, flip to the glossary at the back of the book for an explanation.

1.2 Power Switches

Before you can do anything on your computer, you need to fire it up. You can do that by giving a quick jab to the power switch on your computer's main box. Have a look at the front of your computer to find this. Power buttons will look different depending on which computer you have. However, they will all have the same symbol next to them, so you can spot them easily. This is a circle with a vertical line running through it. Whenever you see this symbol on a computer, you're looking at a power button.

1.2.1 Starting Up

1 First, press the power button on your PC.

2 Press the power button on your monitor.

I can't see the symbol on any of the buttons!

Sometimes the power symbol might be printed on the actual casing of the computer, rather than on the button itself. Very occasionally, you might see the word 'Power' – instead of a symbol – next to the button.

1.3 The Parts of a Computer

Computers come in a variety of shapes and sizes, but they all share a number of common components. In addition to these main parts of your computer, you may have extra peripherals, such as speakers, a printer or a scanner. These extra items enable your computer to complete more tasks, but are not essential for it to work properly. Pictured below are the key items you need for your PC to work as it should.

1 **Base unit**: This is the square box that all the other parts plug into. It contains all the circuitboards, processors and other technical wizardry required for your PC to work.

2 **Monitor**: Also known as a screen or visual display unit (VDU), this is the part of the computer that shows you what is going on, and what you are doing. For example, in a word-processing program, you would see the letters you type appearing on the screen.

3 **Keyboard**: This is what you use to type information into the computer. As well as the basic alphanumeric keys (letters and numbers), you'll also find a range of function keys that help you complete common tasks more quickly.

4 **Mouse**: The mouse is used to point and click on things on the screen. When you move the mouse, a pointer on the screen moves as well. If you press the mouse button while the pointer is on certain icons or buttons, you can run programs or press buttons.

1.4 Using the Mouse

If you've never used a computer mouse before, you might be feeling a bit wary about getting the hang of this strange-looking piece of kit. However, using a mouse is a very intuitive process – you'll soon be clicking around as if you've been using one for years.

The mouse is used to point and click on things on the screen – when you move the mouse, a pointer on the screen moves as well. Pressing the mouse will make things happen on the screen. Usually you'll use the left mouse button to tell the computer where you want to type text, or to find your way around the web.

1.4.1 Use the Mouse

1 Rest the heel of your hand on the desk before your mouse.

2 Hold the mouse with your thumb on the left and your last three fingers on the right side of the mouse.

3 Lightly lay your index finger on the button at the top left of the mouse.

4 Without picking it up or turning it over, move the mouse so that the pointer on the screen moves.

5 Move the mouse pointer to the position you require.

6 Keeping the mouse still, click **lightly** with the index finger on the left button.

What if I'm left-handed?

As with most things in this world, computer mice are set up to be used by right-handed folk. However, most mice will fit just as comfortably in either hand, so you can simply move the mouse onto the other side of your desk.

If you do this, it's a good idea to switch over the functions of the mouse buttons. Normally, the left mouse button does most of the work. If you're holding the mouse in your left hand, it's more comfortable to make the right mouse button the main one. To do this…

1 Click on the Start button at the bottom left of the screen.

2 Click on the Control Panel option on the menu that appears.

3 Click on the Buttons tab at the top of the box that appears.

4 Click in the box next to **Switch primary and secondary buttons**, so it is ticked.

5 Click on the OK button.

1.5 Right Clicking

You'll find your mouse has two main buttons, one on the left and one on the right. Most of the time, you'll be using the left mouse button.

Using the right mouse button will do different things to using the left mouse button. Normally, clicking the right mouse button brings up a list of options on the screen.

Using the right mouse button is called right clicking. Using the left mouse button is simply called clicking.

1.5.1 Right Clicking

1 Move the mouse pointer to the position you require.

2 Position your middle finger on the right mouse button.

3 Keeping the mouse still, click lightly with the middle finger on the right button.

1.6 Double Clicking

A third way to use the mouse is by double clicking. Double clicking just means clicking twice in quick succession with the left mouse button.

You'll usually use a double click when you want to open something that's stored on your computer, such as a document you've saved. Double clicking can be tricky to get the hang of at first, but after a few goes you'll soon get it. You don't have to be lightning fast to do a double click, just make sure you've done the second click within a half-second of the first.

1.6.1 How to Double Click

1 Move the mouse pointer to the position you require.

2 Lightly press your left mouse button twice quickly, taking care to keep your mouse still.

1.6.2 Mouse Pointers

The pointer on the screen gives you an idea of what your mouse can do in the position it is in:

▲	This mouse pointer will appear as you move it around the screen (it can also be used to move things)
I	This mouse pointer will also appear as you move it around the screen, particularly if it is over text. (This shape can be seen when you are about to type text.)
↑	This mouse pointer will show up when you move the pointer over a link on the screen. Links can be clicked to move to a different file on your computer.

1.7 Using the Keyboard

While you'll use the mouse to move around the different areas of your computer, you'll use your keyboard mainly to enter information.

Using a keyboard is much the same as using a typewriter – you just tap the keys with your fingers to type. When you've got a suitable program running on your computer, whatever you type will appear on your screen.

However, there are stacks more keys on your keyboard than you would find on an old-fashioned typewriter. These help you control some of the functions on your computer.

1.7.1 Typing

1 Press the key with the letter or number you require.

2 If you type something by mistake you can use the Backspace key to get rid of one letter at a time. It will remove text from behind (to the left of) your cursor position.

3 Press the Space bar to get spaces between words.

4 Press the Return key to move to a new line in your document.

5 Press the punctuation mark keys to add one of these marks.

As well as the letter and number keys, there are lots more that give added functions to your keyboard. For instance, if you want to type in CAPITAL LETTERS, just use the Caps Lock button. You'll find this on the far left of the keyboard, immediately to the left of the letter A key. You can't miss it – it will have 'Caps Lock' written on it. Handy, that.

The Shift key is positioned directly below Caps Lock. The purpose of this key is to temporarily change what the other keys do. Hold the Shift key down while you want to access the other functions of the keys. For instance, hold down Shift and then press a letter key and you will type a capital letter. Once you let go of the key, your typing will come out in lowercase once again.

1.8.1 How to Type in Capitals

1 Press the Caps Lock key. The Caps Lock light will light up on your keyboard.

2 Start typing.

3 To stop typing in capitals, press the Caps Lock key again.

1.8.2 Typing One Capital at a Time

1 Press and hold the Shift key.

2 Press the letter you require.

3 Release the Shift key.

I can't see the Caps Lock light!

All keyboards are different, and the light that shows your Caps Lock is activated will be in a different place depending on which keyboard you're using. You'll normally find the light at the top-right of your keyboard. However, it may be built into the Caps Lock key itself.

Take a look at your keyboard and you'll notice some of the keys have more than one character printed on them. For instance, look at the key immediately to the left of the Shift key on the right-hand side of your keyboard. This will have a forward slash symbol and also a question mark on it.

To type the lowermost of these symbols (in this case, the forward slash), simply press the key. But to access the uppermost symbol (in this case, the question mark), you need to press and hold down the Shift key while you press the key.

1.9.1 Typing More Punctuation Marks

1 Press and hold the Shift key.

2 Press the key that has the required punctuation mark at the top.

3 Release the Shift key.

Finding other symbols

There are more symbols that can be found on the number keys. For example, the pound sign (£) is at the top of the number 3 key. To type these you will need to use the Shift key.

1.10 Useful Keys

Your keyboard has more than just a bunch of letters and numbers on it. You can also use it to quickly perform common functions (such as opening a help screen, or saving a document).

You can use the cursor keys to move the cursor around the screen. Or you can use command keys, such as Tab or Delete, to quickly make changes to the work you are doing on screen.

Once you get the hang of using these additional keys, you can move around programs on your screen far more quickly than if you rely only on your mouse.

1.10.1 Other Keys

The cursor keys are usually found in a separate group to the bottom-right of all the letters. They can be used to move the position of the cursor. To use a cursor key press the key with the arrow pointing in the direction you wish to move the cursor.

Another way to delete text is using the Delete key (usually found above the cursor keys). Press the Delete key to delete text in front of the cursor position.

The tab key can be used to position text when you are typing letters. When you are looking at a web page it can be used to move from one text box to another. It can usually be found to the left of the letter Q key.

The Function keys are right at the top of the keyboard and can be used as a quick way to access things. For instance, pressing F1 will bring up a help screen in most programs.

Delete is not the same as Backspace

The delete key gets rid of text in front of the cursor position (to the right) and the backspace key gets rid of text behind (to the left of) the cursor position.

1.11　The Number Pad

Most keyboards will have a separate group of keys that can be used for just typing in numbers. This is called the number pad and if you've got one you'll see it on the far right of your keyboard.

To use the numbers on the number pad you must make sure that Num Lock is turned on. Some people like to use the number pad, but using the number keys at the top of the main part of the keyboard has just the same effect.

1.11.1　To Switch Num Lock On...

Press the Num Lock key (the Num Lock light on your keyboard will come on).

1.11.2　To Switch Num Lock Off...

Press the Num Lock key (the Num Lock key will go off).

1.11.3　With Num Lock Switched On...

Press the key with the number you require.

If Num Lock is not on...

...the keys will do different things; for example, pressing 8 will move your cursor up a line.

1.12　Logging On

Once you've started up your computer you will probably see a box asking you to log on. This is especially likely if you're using a computer at work. So, why do you need to log on? Well, the whole point of it is so the computer knows who is using it. It's a bit like typing a PIN number into a cash machine.

Different people may have different levels of access to what is stored on your computer. So, you might be able to access certain files when you log in with your own details, while other files may be blocked from you. Also, the way the computer is set up will be different for different people. By logging on, you ensure the computer displays the right files and loads the correct settings.

1.12.1　Entering your Details

1 Click in the box next to user name.

2 Type in your user name.

3 Click in the box next to Password.

4 Type your password.

5 Click OK.

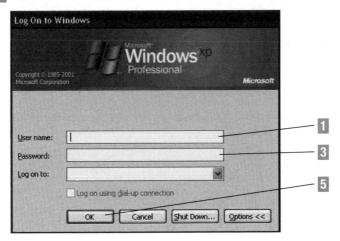

1.12.2 Creating a Password

If this is the first time you have used this particular computer or someone has used another password on the computer you may have to do the following:

1 Click in the box next to New password.

2 Type in your password.

3 Click in the box next to Confirm new password.

4 Type your password again.

5 Click OK.

1.13 Logging Off

If someone else wants to use your computer you need to make sure that they use their own name and password. If they stay logged on as you, they may accidentally change your settings, or gain access to personal information on your computer. Additionally, if they send any emails from the desktop, those messages will be sent with your name on. What you need to do is log off, then have the other person log on as themselves.

Logging off is quicker than shutting down and restarting the computer but still ensures that the next person to use the computer has to enter their own username and password.

1.13.1 Logging Off

1 Click on the Start button.

2 Click on Log Off…

3 Click Log Off.

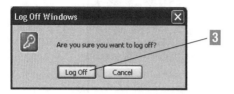

1.13.2 Logging On Again

Just enter your username and password as you would when first starting the computer.

1 Click in the box next to User name.

2 Type your user name.

3 Click in the box before Password.

4 Type your password.

5 Click OK.

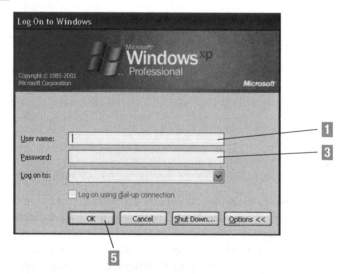

1.14 Shutting Down

Once you've had enough for the day, you'll want to turn off your computer. However, it's not as simple as turning off something like your telly. If you don't close your computer down in the correct way you risk losing some of your work and even damaging the computer.

Before you switch off your computer you must first ensure that it is not still doing anything. It's not always obvious what processes are running on your computer, so the only way to be absolutely sure your PC is no longer doing anything is to use the Shut Down feature. Using this method will ensure that any settings you have changed are saved and that the computer has finished copying all the information you have saved to a safe place.

1.14.1 To Shut Down

1 Click on the Start button.

2 Click on Shut Down.

3 Click on the drop-down menu and click on Shut Down.

4 Click OK.

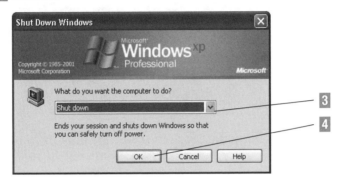

1.14.2 To Restart

1 Click on the Start button.

2 Click on Shut Down.

3 Click on the drop-down menu and click on Restart.

4 Click OK.

Staying safe in a crash

Sometimes your computer might have a funny turn and stop responding. This is normally called a 'crash'. The only thing to do in this case is to restart the computer. But if your computer's crashed, you'll find your mouse pointer is no longer responding to your commands.

The way around this is to press the Ctrl, Alt and Delete keys at the same time. This will bring up a dialog box on which you can click the Shut Down button. Now the Shut Down box will appear, enabling you to choose to shut down or restart the system.

CHAPTER 2

Getting Around the Desktop

2.1 Introduction

Once your computer is loaded up, all the information it contains is at your fingertips.

The first thing you'll see is called the 'desktop'. You'll come across lots of real-world terms such as 'desktop' when you're using a computer – techy types like to use them to make us all feel a bit more at home. What the term actually refers to is what you can see on your screen once the computer is fully booted up. It's from here you can open any program or file stored on your PC.

The key to your desktop is the Start button, which you'll see at the bottom-left of the screen. Using the Start button, you can explore every single item of data stored on your computer. Most of the time, you'll use the Start button to open a new program.

Whenever you do open a program, it will appear in what's called a 'window'. You can have many windows open at once – which means you can have lots of programs and separate files all running at the same time. These windows can be moved around the screen, so if one is in the way, you can move it aside. Alternatively, you can change the size of the windows, or even 'tile' them so they all take up an equal part of the screen.

The easiest way to get around programs is by using the mouse to click on the various menus and toolbars. These give you quick links to commonly used functions, thus speeding up the way you use the program. If you run into any trouble, there's always a Help function you can use to dig up some pointers.

2.2 Starting a Program

A program enables you to communicate with the computer to get it to do a variety of tasks. Programs are specialised to perform particular jobs. For example, if you wanted to write a letter using your computer, you would use a word-processing program. If you wanted to create a budget sheet including a number of calculations, you would need to use a spreadsheet program. A brand new computer will normally come bundled with a range of programs straight out of the box, such as the Microsoft Office software.

2.2.1 Starting a Program

1 Click on the Start button.

2 Click on All Programs.

3 Click on the program you want to start.

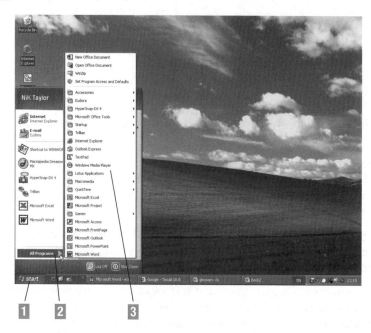

Type of program	What does it do?	Examples
Operating system	Is the software that runs the computer, allowing you to easily start other programs and access your work	Windows, MacOS, Linux
Word processors	Have the same function as a typewriter – for producing letters, reports or other written documents	Word, WordPerfect
Spreadsheets	Tables containing text and figures, which you can perform calculations on. Spreadsheets are usually used for budgets, statistics and so on	Excel, Lotus 1-2-3
Databases	These store information, e.g. the names and addresses of all your clients	Access, FileMaker Pro
Presentation tools	To support presentations by allowing you to produce slides or handouts	PowerPoint
Desktop publishing (DTP)	For producing magazines, newsletters etc.	Quark, PageMaker, Publisher
Multimedia applications	Used for producing multimedia presentations, e.g. websites, animations, videos	Dreamweaver, FrontPage, Flash

2.3 Parts of a Window

Every task you perform on your computer will open in a box called a window. For instance, when you open Word, a window appears on the screen containing the software. You then work inside the window. It is possible to have many windows open at once, so you can run lots of different programs and files at the same time, switching between them as you need to.

1 Title bar: This tells you which program you're using and which file is open.

2 Menu bar: You use the menu bar to access the main functions of a program. You'll always see a menu bar in this position on the program. Clicking on any of the menus brings up a list of options.

3 Toolbar: Toolbars contain a number of buttons. Each of these buttons has a different function – clicking on them activates the function.

4 Minimise: Clicking on this button makes the program window disappear. It can be brought back by clicking on the relevant button on the taskbar.

5 Maximise/restore: This button has two functions, depending on how the window looks. If the window is only filling part of the screen, clicking here will make it fill the whole screen. The button will then change, so clicking it will then make the window revert to its original size.

6 Close: Click on this button to close down the program you're using.

Screenshot provided courtesy of Happy (www.happy.co.uk).

This is the first screen you'll see once your computer has started. It can be customised to look how you want and make it easier for you to do your work. Whenever you open a program, it will open in a window on top of the desktop, so you won't be able to see the desktop any more.

However, the desktop will always be present in the background so if you ever need to access something that's stored on there you just need to minimise the windows you have already opened. See the next section to find out how to do this.

1 **Icons**: These are shortcuts to files and programs stored on your computer. Double clicking on any of these icons will open them.

2 **Background**: You can have any picture you like set as your desktop background

3 **Start button**: The simplest way to open any of the programs on your computer. Click on the Start button and you'll see a menu of options.

4 **Taskbar**: Listed here are all the programs and files currently open. Click on any of these to bring that program's window to the front of the screen.

5 **Quick Launch Toolbar**: Shortcuts to commonly used programs are stored here. Click once on any of these icons to open its associated program.

6 **System Tray**: Here you can see a list of all the processes currently running on your system.

7 **Clock**: Shows you the time. If it's wrong, double click on the clock to change it.

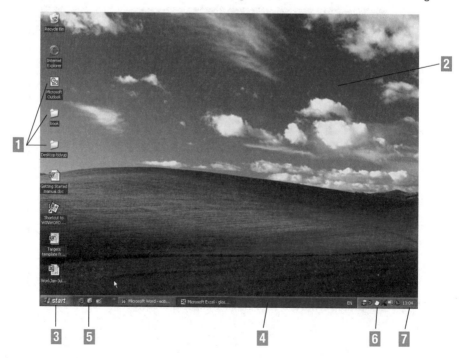

Switching from one program to another

You can have lots of programs running at the same time on your computer. The quickest way to switch between them is to use the taskbar at the bottom of the screen. All the programs currently open will be listed here – just click on the button for the program you want to move to.

2.5 Working with Windows

Computers these days are powerful machines indeed, and they're capable of running lots of different programs at the same time. This is great news for saving time, but it can get confusing if you've got tons of windows open all over the screen – which is where maximising and minimising comes in.

At the top right of every window you open, you'll see a few buttons. You can click on these to make the window bigger, smaller, or to hide it in the background until you want to use it again.

2.5.1 Minimising a Window

1 Click on the Minimise button.

2 Click on the Maximise button in the task bar to bring it back.

3 Click on the Close button to close the screen.

By kind permission of Google (www.google.co.uk).

2.5.2 Maximising a Window

1 Click on the Maximise button.

2 Click on the Restore button to return it to its previous size.

2.5.3 Closing a Window

1 Click the X at the top right of the window.

2.6 Moving and Resizing Windows

If one window is in the way of another, you've got a couple of options. You can either move one of the windows, or resize them. To do either of these things, you'll need to use a handy technique known as 'click and drag'. What this means is that you click with the left mouse button, and keep that button held down. Now, drag the mouse so the pointer moves to the position you want, then let go of the mouse button.

2.6.1 Moving Windows

1 Position the mouse pointer over the title bar of the window.

2 Click and drag the window to its new position. You'll see an outline of where the window will now appear once you've moved it.

By kind permission of Google (www.google.co.uk).

2.6.2 Resizing Windows

1 Position the mouse pointer on the very edge of the window. The pointer will change shape to look like a two-headed arrow.

2 Click and drag to change the shape of the window.

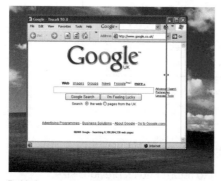

By kind permission of Google (www.google.co.uk).

If you position your mouse at a corner you can resize in both directions at once (height and width).

2.7 Choosing Menu Commands

Menus will help you control the program you are using. You can see which menus are available to you by looking at the menu bar at the top of the screen.

To see the options contained within a menu, simply click on its name. You'll find the options are personalised to the way you work, so each menu only displays the options you use most often. This will save you time normally, but if you need to see all the options on a menu, simply double click on its name. Alternatively, you can click on the down-pointing double-headed arrows at the bottom of the menu.

2.7.1 Choose a Command From the Menu

1 Click a menu name on the menu bar.

2 Click on the double-headed arrows if necessary.

3 Click on the option you require.

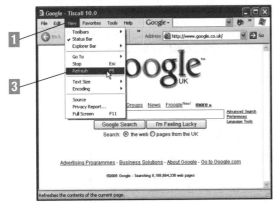

By kind permission of Google (www.google.co.uk).

Using sub-menus

Sometimes a menu will contain sub-menus. This is where a menu option has another menu attached to it. You'll be able to see if this is the case, as the option will have an arrow at the end of it. Hold the mouse pointer over this option and the sub-menu will appear.

2.8 Choosing Toolbar Commands

A super-quick way to get things done in any program is to use the toolbar buttons. The buttons on a toolbar enable you to perform a range of common commands with just one click – so they're generally a far quicker way to get things done than clicking through tons of menus.

The toolbars for the program you're using will be displayed at the top of its window. Bear in mind you might not be able to see all the buttons if the window is not maximised. You can tell if that's the case as there will be two arrows at the end of the toolbar. Click on the arrows to see the other options available.

2.8.1 Using a Toolbar

1 Click on the button you want to use.

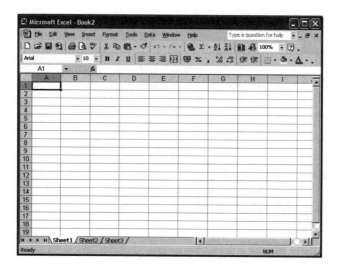

2.9 | Tile and Cascade Windows

Sometimes you might need to be able to view a couple of windows at the same time – for instance, if you're copying from one window into another. A quick way to do this is to tile the windows open on your screen.

Windows can be tiled horizontally or vertically. See below for the difference between the two options.

If you want to keep your windows at near full-screen size, but want them to be more easily accessible, try using the cascade option. This lays all the windows on top of each other in an overlapping pattern, so you can quickly skip between them by clicking on the title bars.

2.9.1 | Tile Windows

1 Position the mouse pointer on a blank area of the taskbar.

2 Click the right-hand mouse button.

3 Click on the tile windows option you require from the menu that appears (you can choose to tile the windows horizontally or vertically).

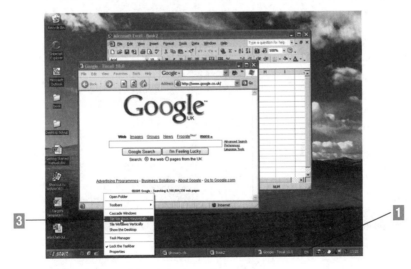

By kind permission of Google (www.google.co.uk).

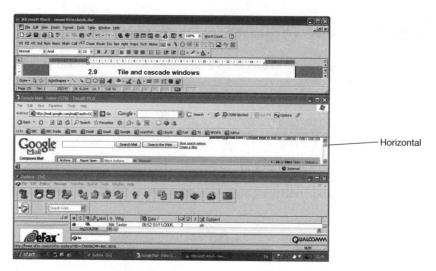

By kind permission of Google (www.google.co.uk).

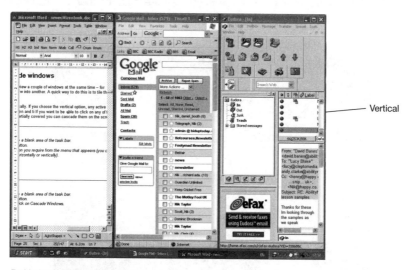

By kind permission of Google (www.google.co.uk).

Top tiling

Tiling is only really useful if you have a limited number of active windows. It works best if you have just two windows, which will then get half the screen each, or if you have four, when they will all be tiled as quarter screen size (see image).

By kind permission of Google (www.google.co.uk).

2.9.2 Cascade Windows

1 Position the mouse pointer on a blank area of the taskbar.

2 Click the right-hand mouse button.

3 On the menu that appears, click on Cascade Windows.

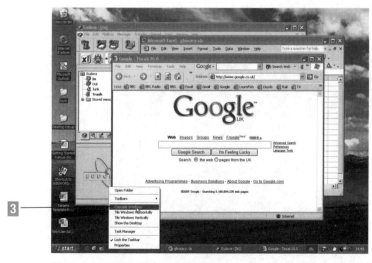

By kind permission of Google (www.google.co.uk).

By kind permission of Google (www.google.co.uk).

2.10 Using Windows Help

Need a hand? If you've got a question about how to use your computer, you can use Microsoft's built-in Windows Online Help system. Using this, you can look through a pre-set list of help topics, or use the search feature to find exactly what you're after. Perhaps the easiest way to get through all the options is to use the Index feature.

2.10.1 Get Help Using Windows Help

1 Click on the Start button.

2 Click on the Help and Support option.

3 Click on the help topic you require from the list on the left.

4 Click on each link to get through to the help section you require.

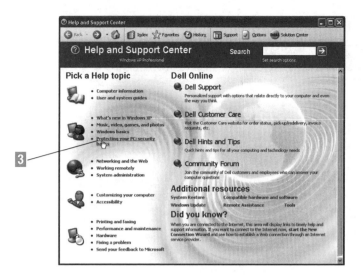

2.10.2 Use the Search Function

1 Start Windows Help.

2 Click inside the Search box and type in what you're looking for.

3 Click on the green arrow button.

4 Click on the help link you require.

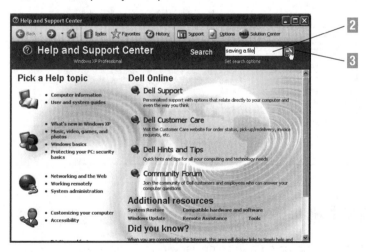

2.10.3 Use the Index Function

1 Start Windows Help.

2 Click on the Index button at the top of the box.

3 Double click on the help topic you require.

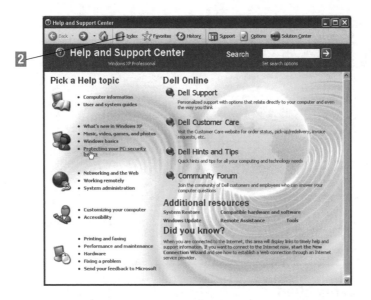

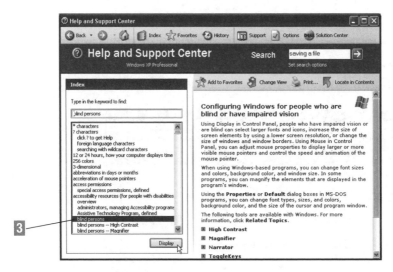

2.11 Files and Folders

All the information on your computer will be stored as some type of file. There will be lots of different files on your computer. For instance, if you write a letter in Microsoft Word it will be stored as a Word document file type.

The simplest way to think of your computer's filing system is as an ordinary filing cabinet...

- The whole of the filing cabinet is your computer.

- The drawers in the filing cabinet are known as **DRIVES**.

- **DRIVES** are represented by letters of the alphabet (for example, your hard drive will probably be denoted by the letter C).

- Inside the drawers are **FOLDERS** that hold your documents.

- Inside some of the folders may be **SUB-FOLDERS** to make things more organised.

- Inside the folders are the pieces of paper that you have written on, known as **FILES**. Word files are known as *documents*.

2.11.1 About File Types

Each different type of file, (e.g. Word document, Excel spreadsheet) has three letters associated with it, called the filename extension. The extension for a type of file lets Windows know what type of file it is, so it knows what icon to display and what program to open the file in.

Underneath the icon for the file you will see the name of the file. Depending on your computer's settings, you may see the name followed by a full stop and then the filename extension (see the Using Windows Explorer section to find out how to change this setting).

Some of the filename extensions you might see…

.doc Excel spreadsheet	Microsoft Word document	.xls	Microsoft
.ppt (e.g. Notepad file)	Microsoft PowerPoint presentation	.txt	Plain text
.mdb Explorer web page	Microsoft Access database	.htm	Internet

2.12 Using Windows Explorer

Windows Explorer is a handy little program you can use to look around the whole of your computer. Once you open it you can see all the drives on your PC. By selecting these, you can look inside and find out which files are stored where.

The screen is divided into two panes. The left-hand side shows the folders on your computer. The right-hand pane represents the contents of the selected item in the left pane. If you click on a folder in its left pane its contents will appear in the right pane.

2.12.1 Opening Windows Explorer

1 Click on the Start button.

2 Click on All Programs.

3 Click on Accessories.

4 Click on Windows Explorer.

A quicker way!

You can open Window Explorer using only the keyboard…

1 Hold down the Windows key (this has a picture of the Windows logo on it and is between the Ctrl and Alt keys).

2 Press the E key.

2.12.2 Expanding and Collapsing

You can expand and collapse the hierarchical view of the left pane to see more or less detail…

1 **Expanding**: If you see a plus (+) by an item in the left pane then it has an additional folder within it. To display, just click on its plus (+).

2 **Collapsing**: If you see a minus by an object then you can hide its contents by clicking on its minus (–).

2.12.3 Looking in a Drive or Folder

1 Click on the drive or folder in the left-hand pane (the contents will be displayed in the right-hand pane).

2.12.4 Opening a Folder in the Right-Hand Pane

1 Double click the folder you wish to open (in the right-hand pane).

Showing file extensions

The default settings in Windows prevent the file extension from being shown at the end of a filename. If you want to change this, it's quite easy...

1 Open Windows Explorer (see section 2.12.1).

2 Click on the Tools menu.

3 Click on the Folder Options option.

4 Click on the View tab.

5 Scroll down the list and click on the **Hide extensions for known file types** option, so it is no longer ticked.

6 Click OK.

2.12.5 Deleting a file

When you delete a file, it is sent to the Recycle Bin. If you change your mind about deleting the file, you can bring it back from the bin later.

1 Select the file(s) or folder(s) you want to delete.

2 Press the Delete key.

2.12.6 Restoring files from the Recycle Bin

1 Double click the Recycle Bin icon on the desktop.

2 Select the file(s) or folder(s) to be restored.

3 Click the File menu.

4 Click Restore.

2.13 Using My Computer

Another way to look through your computer's files is to open the My Computer feature. Once you open My Computer, you'll be able to browse through all the drives connected to your computer, in a similar way to when you use Windows Explorer.

You'll also see a list of shortcuts on the left of the window, which enable you to quickly open features such as the Control Panel.

2.13.1 Opening My Computer

1 Click on the Start button.

2 Click on the My Computer option.

3 Double click on a drive to view its contents.

4 Double click on a folder to view its contents.

5 Double click on a file to open it.

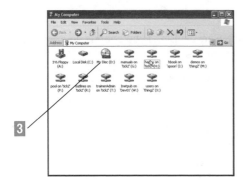

Not sure where something is?

Click on the big Search button at the top of the My Computer box. The search wizard will now appear on the left of the box (this wizard looks like a small dog…!). Go through the search wizard to find the files you're after.

Moving back and forward

When viewing a folder in the My Computer screen, you can move to the previous folder by clicking on the Back button at the top left. Return to the sub-folder by clicking the Forward button.

Copying or moving files

To make a copy of a file or move it to another folder, first right click on the file. Now click on Cut (to move the file) or Copy (to make a copy). Right click inside the destination folder and click on Paste to complete the process.

CHAPTER 3

Starting with Programs

3

3.1 Introduction

If you want to get anything done on a computer, you'll need to use a program. Also known as software, programs can help you do anything from creating a business letter to printing off your holiday snaps. Of course, all computer programs have different functions, so you'll find they all work in different ways. However, there are some common threads to using any program you'll find on your computer.

Opening a program will always be done in the same way, and with just a few clicks of the mouse. You'll generally use the Start button to do this. Once you've opened the program, you then use it to open either a new or existing file. This process is the same with all the common programs, so once you know how to open a file on one program, you know how to do it on all of them.

Once you start working on a file, there's one very big golden rule. **Always** save your work. If you're half-way through something and the power fails, you run the risk of losing everything you've been working on. Saving your work regularly protects you from that, because even if the worst happens you won't lose too much of your work. Saving also serves another purpose, as it enables you to store a copy of your file in a format other programs can understand.

Computers can seem hugely complicated when you first start using them, but the good thing is that all the common programs work in a similar way. So if you want to print off a document, save some work or open an existing file, you'll do it in more or less the same way no matter which program you are using.

3.2 Opening Microsoft Office Programs

The Start menu is your passport to opening anything on your computer. Using this button, you can open whole programs, aim for particular files or run a search for items stored on your computer.

A lot of the work you do on your computer will be done in Microsoft Office. This package of computer programs includes Word (which you use for word-processing) and Excel (which is used to create spreadsheets in which you can do stacks of complicated calculations easily).

3.2.1 Opening an Office Program

1 Click on the Start button.

2 Click on All Programs.

3 Hold the mouse pointer over the Microsoft Office option.

4 Click on the name of the program you want to open.

3.2.2 Opening Internet Explorer

1 Click on the Start button.

2 Click on All Programs.

3 Click on the Microsoft Internet Explorer option.

A really quick way

You can use the Quick Launch icons to open commonly used programs with just one click on the mouse. The Quick Launch icons can be found on the right of the Start button. Just click on the icon for the program you want to open. Hold the mouse pointer over any of the icons to find out what program it is for.

3.3   Creating a New Document

When you open a program, a new document will usually open automatically on the screen. However, you'll need to open your own new documents regularly as well.

The process is roughly the same no matter what program you're using. It's quickest if you click on the icons, but these vary from program to program. You will always be able to create a new document by using the menus.

3.3.1   How to Create a New Document

1 Click on the File menu.

2 Click on the New option.

A new shortcut

You can use a keyboard shortcut to create a new document in most Windows programs. Hold down the Ctrl key then press N.

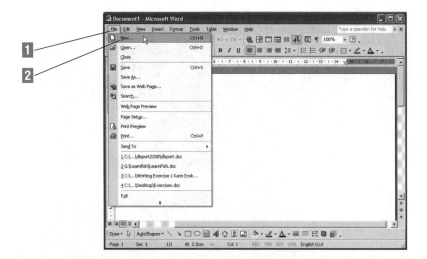

Working with Text

Microsoft Word serves one main purpose – to enable you to quickly create letters and other text-based documents. In order to do this, it needs to know what text you want to add. There are all sorts of nifty tricks and gimmicks you can use in Word to make your project look like a work of art, but the gist of the whole program is quite simple – just get typing!

Once the main screen is open, keep an eye out for a blinking vertical line. This is the insertion point, and it shows you where text will appear when you start typing. Click on any part of the text in your document to move the insertion point to that place.

3.4.1 Adding Text

1 Click on the place on the document where you want to type.

2 Start typing using the keyboard.

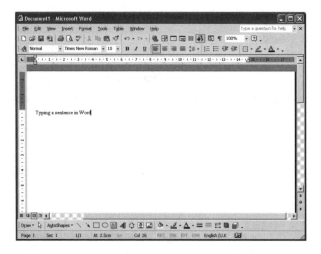

3.4.2 Removing Text

1 Click to the immediate right of the text you want to remove.

2 Press the Backspace key until the text has gone.

3.4.3 Using Overtype Mode

1 Press the Insert key to turn on overtype mode.

2 Anything you type will now overwrite what was there before.

3 Press the Insert key again to turn off overtype.

Click and type

Word is normally set up so you can only move the insertion point to a place where there is already text. However, you can move the insertion point to blank areas of the document by using the Click and Type feature. Just double click on the place in the document where you want the insertion point to appear.

3.5 Saving a Document

For the sake of your own sanity and that of those around you it's important to save your work often. When it comes to computers, there's nothing more hair-tearingly frustrating than losing all your work from the past few hours because your computer's crashed and you'd forgotten to save your work.

When you save a document, you store a copy of it in its current state somewhere on your computer. So, any time you want to go back to the file, you can carry on from where you left off. Saving is quick and easy to do – so make sure you don't forget!

3.5.1 Saving a New Document

1 Click on the File menu.

2 Click on Save As.

3 Click on the Save in box and select the location for the file to be saved in.

4 Click in the File name box and type a name for the file.

5 Click on the Save button.

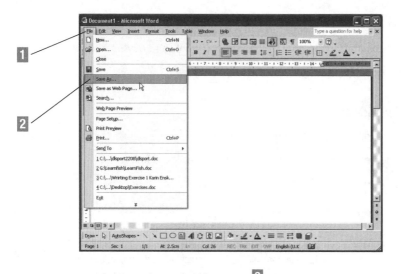

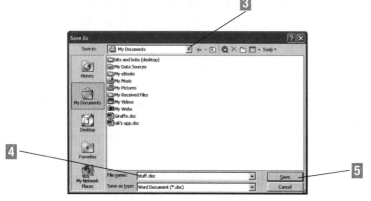

3.5.2 Saving an Existing Document

1 Click on the Save icon.

A handy shortcut

You can save documents quickly using a keyboard shortcut. Just hold down the Ctrl key, then press S.

3.5.3 Opening a Saved File

1 Click the File menu.

2 Click on Open.

3 Double click on the folder containing your file.

4 Double click on the file.

3.6 Saving into Another File Format

Each program on your computer saves files in a particular way so it can understand them when it comes to open them again. You don't have to give that process a second thought – it happens automatically whenever you save.

However, you'll sometimes want to make it possible for a file to be opened by a program that's different from the one that created it. In this case, you have to save the file using a slightly different method.

This is called saving the file in a different format. For instance, you can save an Excel spreadsheet in the Word document format. The spreadsheet can then be opened in Word.

3.6.1 Saving in a Different Format

1 Click on the File menu.

2 Click on Save As.

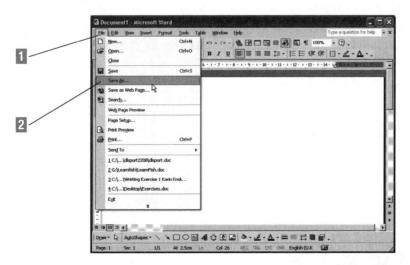

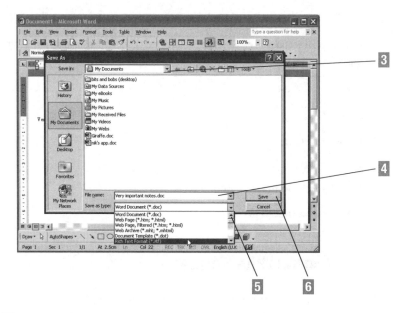

3 Click on the Save in box and change the location for the file to be saved in, if necessary.

4 Click in the File name box and change the filename, if necessary.

5 Click in the Save as Type box and select the file format you want to save it as.

6 Click on the Save button.

3.7 Printing

Once upon a time, printers were hulking beige boxes that took about half a day to print out a black and white letter. These days, if you've got a printer attached to your PC, it's likely to be a svelte-looking piece of kit that's capable of whipping out a camera-load of full-colour pictures in a couple of minutes.

If you do have a functioning printer attached to your PC, you can make print-outs of anything you see on the computer screen with just a couple of clicks of the mouse.

3.7.1 Print

1 Click on the File menu.

2 Click on the Print option.

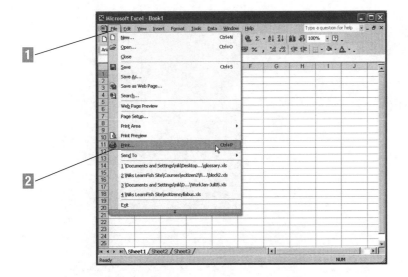

Speedy printing

The quickest way to print out something is to simply click on the Print icon. This will have an image of a printer on it – something like this…

Alternatively, you can use another keyboard shortcut – press the Ctrl and P keys.

3.7.2 Checking on Print Progress

1 Click on the Start button.

2 Click on the Control Panel.

3 Double click on Printers and Faxes.

4 Double click on the printer you're using (the printer you are using will have a tick next to it).

5 Any documents you have waiting to be printed will be displayed in the window that's opened.

6 The Status column shows you what stage of the printing process the document has reached.

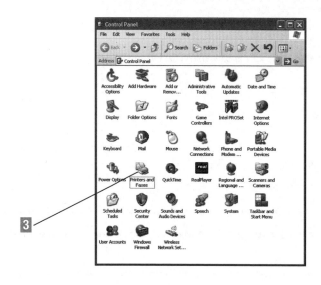

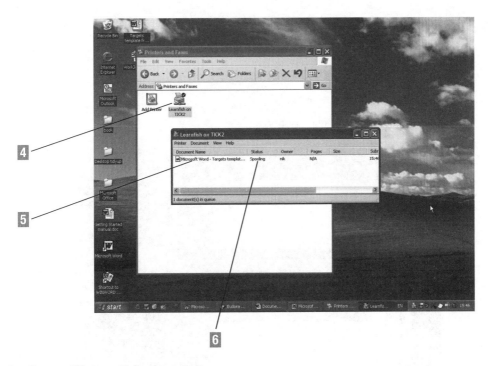

3.7.3 Cancelling a Printing Job

1 Open the printer window as above.

2 Click on the document you want to cancel.

3 Click on the Document menu.

4 Click on the Cancel option.

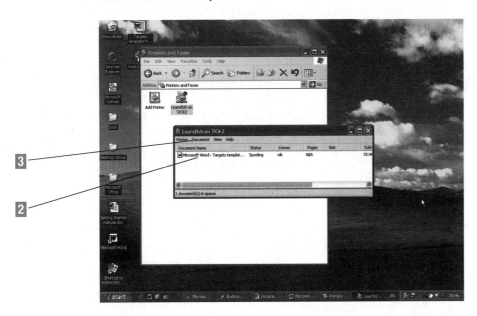

3.7.4 Pausing a Print Job

1 Open the printer window as above.

2 Click on the document you want to pause.

3 Click on the Document menu.

4 Click on the Pause Printing option.

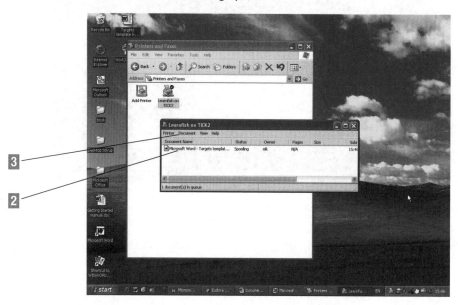

Restarting printing

Just follow the same steps as for pausing a print job!

3.8 Closing Down

When you've finished using a program, you need to close it down. Before you can do that, you need to make sure you've saved and closed all the work you've been doing with it. Don't worry if you think you might forget. If you try to close down a program without having saved all the work you've done, a reminder will pop up on the screen to alert you.

3.8.1 Closing a Document

1 Click on the lower of the two X buttons at the top right of the program window.

Why can't I close down my document?

If you've made some changes to your file since you last saved it, a message will appear when you try to close it. If you want to save the changes you've made, click on the Yes button. If, on the other hand, you want all your recent work to flutter away into the ether, never to be seen again, click on No.

If you're all of a panic because you didn't want to close the document at all, simply click on the Cancel button.

3.8.2 Closing a Program

1 Click on the X button at the very top right of the program window.

CHAPTER 4

Internet Basics

4.1 Introduction

People often use the terms 'Internet' and 'World Wide Web' to describe the same thing – but they are in fact different. The World Wide Web (normally shortened to WWW or web) is simply a part of the Internet. It presents information from the Internet in a way we can use – websites. The Internet as a whole is the physical structure of computers that are all networked together. It has two main parts, the web and email.

Using the web, you can find information, shop for goods, download software, and much more. Using email, you can send messages instantly to anywhere on the planet.

To use the web, you need a web browser. By far the most popular is Microsoft Internet Explorer, though several others, such as Mozilla Firefox and Opera, are rapidly gaining legions of devotees. Newcomers to the web are most likely to use Internet Explorer (IE), but all browsers work in a largely similar way.

Using them, you can access any website in the world, so long as you know its address. If you don't know its address, you can find it out by using a search engine – a special type of website which looks through the Internet to find what you want. Once you've accessed a site, you move around it by clicking on parts of the site known as links.

Browsers also offer other features, such as the option to save lists of your favourite sites, print out web pages, or save pages to your computer's hard drive.

4.2 Internet Explorer Screen

To view web pages on your computer, you need a crafty piece of software known as a web browser. There's no doubting the market-leader in terms of web browsers – it's Microsoft's Internet Explorer. Though a handful of other browsers are gaining ground, Internet Explorer (IE) is still used by the vast majority of Internet users. There are a wide range of features on the IE screen but, as usual, there are a few key ones that you'll use more than others.

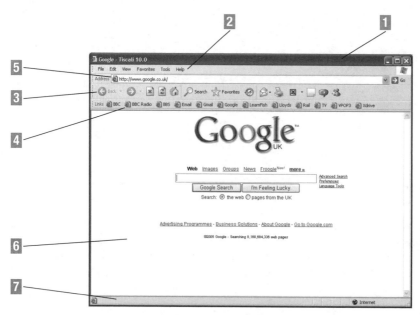

By kind permission of Google (www.google.co.uk).

1 **Title bar**: Gives you the title of the web page you are currently viewing.

2 **Menu bar**: Gives you access to all the commands available in Internet Explorer.

3 **Standard buttons toolbar**: Click on any of the buttons for a quick way of performing that particular command.

4 **Links bar**: You can choose to fill this bar up with links to sites you regularly visit.

5 **Address bar**: Use this to type in the address of the site you want to visit.

6 **Web page**: The main window is where the web page you're viewing appears.

7 **Status bar**: Displays messages such as the progress on connecting to a website. The right-hand side will indicate the security settings for the web page you are looking at.

4.2.1 Starting Internet Explorer

1 Click on the Start button.

2 Click on the All Programs option.

3 Click on Internet Explorer.

4.3 Going to a Web Address

Every page on the Internet has its own address (impress the next person you meet by referring to this by its technical term – Uniform Resource Locator, or URL for short). Typing the address of a page into your web browser takes you straight there.

If you're not used to using web addresses, they can simply look like a lot of gobbledegook. But all this information tells the browser where to look for the page you want. For example, consider the address http://www.bbc.co.uk/news.

The first part (http://) tells the browser what computer language the page is coded in. Don't worry about that – it will be the same for almost all the sites you visit.

The second part (www.bbc.co.uk) is the domain name. This is the main address for the site. You can learn something about the site by looking at its domain. For instance, the .co.uk in our example shows the site is a UK company. A site with .org.uk would be a UK organisation. Most of the time, simply typing in this part of the address will take you to the site.

The final part of the address (/news), is the path. This tells the browser which particular page on that site to look for.

4.3.1 Using the Address Bar

1 Type the address into the address bar.

2 Press the Return key on the keyboard.
or
Click on the Go button at the end of the address bar.

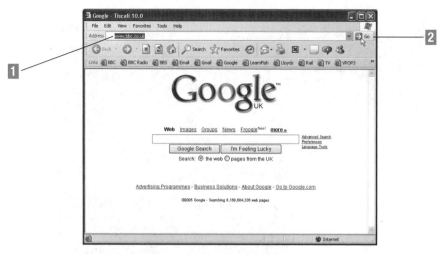

By kind permission of Google (www.google.co.uk).

4.3.2 Accessing Previous Addresses

1 Click on the down arrow at the end of the address bar.

2 Click on the address you want to go to.

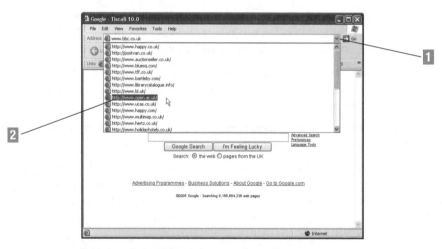

By kind permission of Google (www.google.co.uk).

4.3.3 Using the Button Bar

1 **Back**: Click here to go back to the previous page.

2 **Forward**: Click to go forward to the next page.

3 **Stop**: Stop the page loading onto your computer.

4 **Refresh**: Reload the page you're looking at.

5 **Home**: Go to the home page set on the browser.

6 **Search**: Go to the browser's set search engine.

7 **Favorites**: Displays the Favorites list.

8 **History**: Displays the history of accessed websites.

9 **Email**: Read or send email.

10 **Print**: Print the page you're currently looking at.

11 **Edit**: Click on the down arrow to choose a package with which to edit this page.

12 **Discussion**: Opens the discussion toolbar.

13 **Extra**: Additional buttons that may be added.

Auto-filling web addresses

There's a quick way to enter web addresses that end in .com. Just type in the middle part of the address, e.g. microsoft, then hold down the Ctrl key and press Return. Internet Explorer will automatically add all the extra parts of the address to take you to http://www.microsoft.com.

Using AutoComplete

Internet Explorer will often fill in your web addresses for you. If you start typing an address that looks like one you've visited before, IE will pop up a list of addresses that match. This is the browser's AutoComplete function. You can use the up and down cursor keys on the keyboard to select the address you want from the list. When the correct one is highlighted, press the Return key.

4.4 Using Links

Links make it easy to get from one web page to another. A link (properly known as a hyperlink) is simply a part of a web page which, when you click on it, tells the browser to go to another page. Way back when, in the early days of the Net, links were easy to spot. They were all underlined, blue text. Many links still look like that, but they can also be different colours of text, buttons or even pictures.

However, there's one easy way to spot a link and that's to keep an eye on your mouse pointer. Move your mouse pointer around a web page and whenever it turns into a hand with a pointing finger, you've found a link. Some links take you to a file, such as a movie or sound clip. You can save these to your hard drive by using the right mouse button.

4.4.1 Using a Link

1 Hold the mouse pointer over the link until it turns to a pointing hand and the link changes colour.

2 Click on the link.

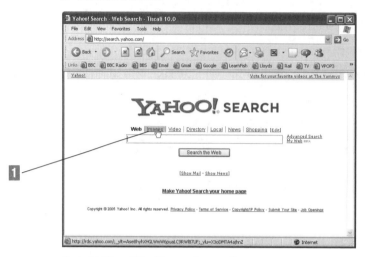

Screenshot from Yahoo! (www.yahoo.co.uk).

4.4.2 Saving From a Link

1 Hold the mouse pointer over the link until it turns to a pointing hand.

2 Right click on the link.

3 Click on Save Target As.

4 Choose a save location and click on the Save button.

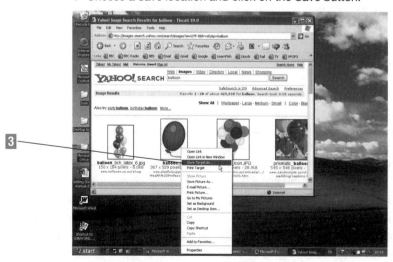

Screenshot from of Yahoo! (www.yahoo.co.uk).

The main page of any website is known as the 'home' page. This is where you'll find the links for all the other pages on the site. To return to the main page, just click on the 'home' link which you'll see somewhere on the page (normally near the top).

4.5 Clearing Your History

Whenever you load a page into Internet Explorer, it makes a little note of it. This can be helpful as it can make getting around the Net much quicker (see section 4.3, Going to a Web Address). However, this information is open to anyone using your computer and you might sometimes not want Explorer to display a record of all the sites you've visited. Perhaps you don't want someone in the family knowing you've been sorting their surprise birthday party online, or maybe you just want to keep your love of geeky Star Trek sites a secret. Whatever, it's easy to delete your list of browsed sites.

4.5.1 Clearing Your History

1 Click on the Tools menu.

2 Click on Internet Options.

3 Click on the General tab.

4 Click on the Clear History button.

5 Click Yes on the dialog box that appears.

6 Click on the OK button.

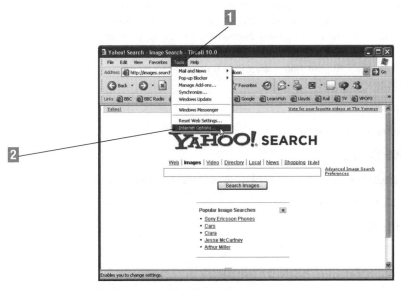

Screenshot from Yahoo! (www.yahoo.com).

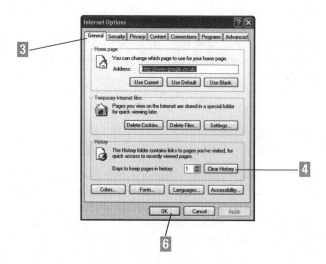

Viewing your history

If you want to see your list of recently visited sites, you simply need to open the History. To do this, press the Ctrl and H keys while you looking at an Internet Explorer window.

The History sidebar will open on the left of the window. Just click on any of the links inside it to go back to that page.

4.6 Setting Your Home Page

The home page is the first page you see when you open your browser up. When you start using Internet Explorer, the home page will be set to something ever-so-useful but interminably dull, such as the Microsoft home page. Happily, you can change the home page to anything you like, so whenever you fire up the web you'll see your favourite page. You can also zip back to your home page any time you like by clicking on the Home button on the IE toolbar.

1. Click on the Tools menu.

2. Click on Internet Options.

3. Click on the General tab.

4. Type the address of the site you want as your home page into the address box.

5. Click on the Apply button.

6. Click on the OK button.

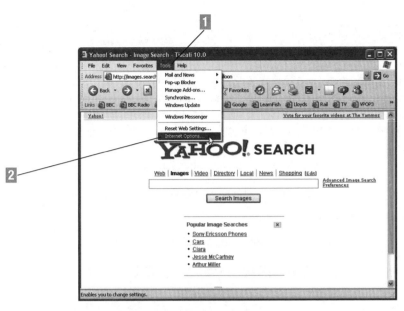

Screenshot from Yahoo! (www.yahoo.com).

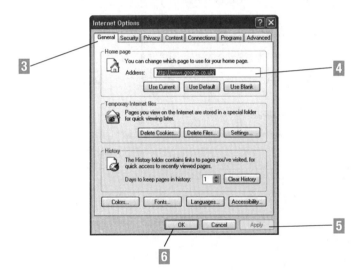

A handy shortcut

To head to your home page quickly, press the Alt and Home keys on your keyboard.

4.7 | Using Search Engines

Until you've visited a website for the first time, you're unlikely to know its address. You could guess, of course, and you might get lucky. Once you get the hang of web addresses, it's quite easy to work out that the BBC site is www.bbc.co.uk and the Microsoft address is www.microsoft.co.uk. But unless you already know the address for B&Q, for instance, how are you going to know that you need to go to www.diy.com? You need a bit of help. That's where search engines come in.

1 Click inside the search box of the search engine you're using.

2 Type in some keywords that describe what you want to look for.

3 Click on the Search the Web button.

4 Click on the link for the site you want from the results that appear.

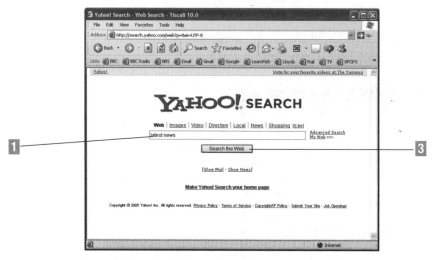

Screenshot from Yahoo! (www.yahoo.com).

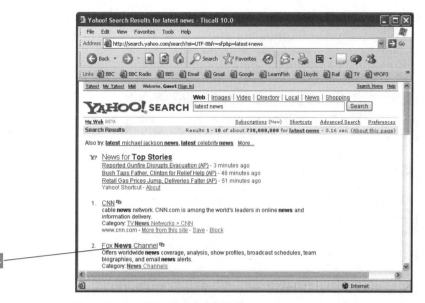

Screenshot from Yahoo! (www.yahoo.com).

Refining your search results

You can use symbols to improve your search results. If you want to search for a particular phrase, you'll get better results if you enclose the phrase in quote marks – e.g. "fish and chips". If you want to exclude websites with a certain word, put a minus sign in front of that word – e.g. football -american. See pages 107–22 for more on using search engines.

4.8 Setting up a Favorites List

Everyone's got their favourites. If you're a football fan, you'll visit the site of your team much more often than you will that of their local rivals. If you like to keep on top of the news, you may spend more time reading the major news-gatherer sites than you do on the online pages of the local rag.

The trouble is, unless you've got a brain the size of a small planet, you're not going to be able to remember the addresses of all your top sites. Time to create a list of your favourites. Once you've done that, you can get to your top sites with just a couple of clicks of the mouse.

4.8.1 Adding a Favorite

1 Go to the site you want to save as a favourite.

2 Click on the Favorites menu.

3 Click on Add to Favorites.

4 Make sure you can see the list of Favorites folders. If not, click on the Create in button.

5 Click on the New Folder button, type in a name for the folder and click on the OK button.
or
Click on the folder in which you want to save the favourite site.

6 Click on the OK button.

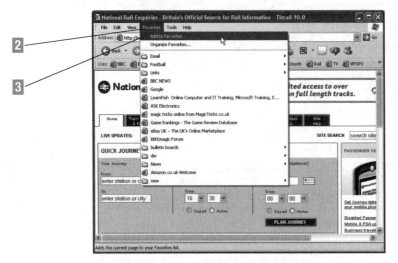

Screenshot from National Rail Enquiries (www.nationalrail.co.uk).

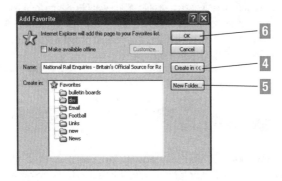

4.8.2 Using Favorites

1 Click on the Favorites menu.

2 Hold the mouse pointer over the folder containing the favourite you want.

3 Click on the site.

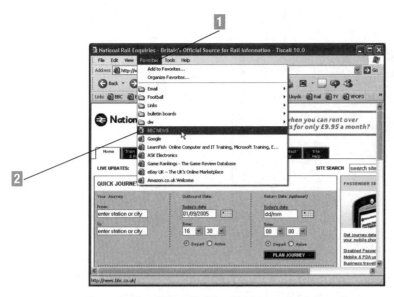

Screenshot from National Rail Enquiries (www.nationalrail.co.uk).

4.8.3 Deleting Favorites

1 Click on the Favorites menu.

2 Click on Organize Favorites.

3 Click on the folder containing the site you want to delete from the list.

4 Click on the site you want to delete.

5 Click on the Delete button.

6 Click on Yes.

7 Click on Close.

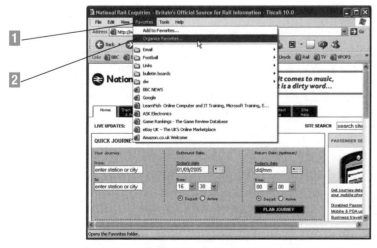

Screenshot from National Rail Enquiries (www.nationalrail.co.uk).

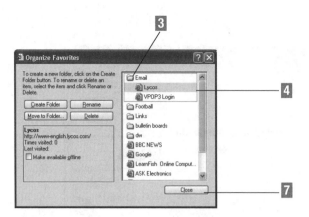

4.9 Saving Web Pages

It's not always practical or possible to go online whenever you want to. If there's something on the Net you need constant access to, you can make a copy on your hard drive. If what you want to copy is simply a chunk of text, it's easy enough to copy and paste it into a word processing document. If you need more than that, you can save a copy of an entire web page.

4.9.1 Copying and Pasting From the Web

1 Select the text you want to copy.

2 Right click on the text.

3 Click on the Copy option.

4 Open a new document in a word-processing document such as Word.

5 Click on the document.

6 Click on the Edit menu and click on the Paste option.

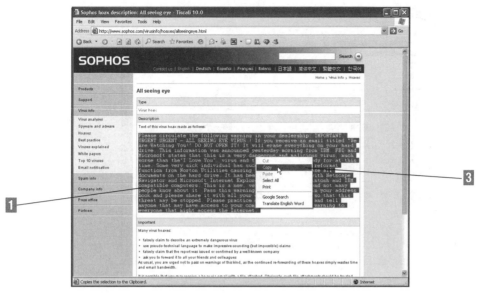

By kind permission of Sophos (www.sophos.com).

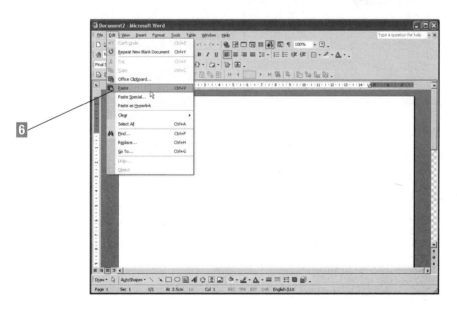

4.9.2 Saving an Entire Web Page

1 Open the page you want to save.

2 Click on the File menu.

3 Click on Save as.

4 Choose a location in which to save the file.

5 Click on the Save button.

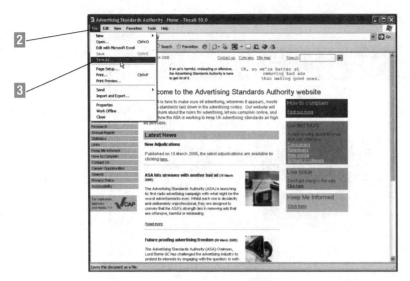

Copyright of the Advertising Standards Authority (www.asa.org.uk).

4.9.3 Saving an image from the Net

1 Right click on the image.

2 Click on Save picture as.

3 Choose a folder in which to save the image.

4 Click on the Save button.

4.10 Printing Web Pages

You've got a number of options when printing out web pages. If you want, you can take a look at a preview of how the page will print before you send it through. You can also choose to print only certain pages from the site, or to print more copies.

Yonks ago, some sites used to use things called frames, which split up a web page into separate sections. Such sites do still exist but they're about as common as purple polar bears. Nevertheless, you can also use the print options to print out just one frame from a page.

4.10.1 Printing a Web Page

1 Click on the File menu.

2 Click on the Print option.

3 Adjust the options as required.

4 Click on the Print button.

Copyright of the Advertising Standards Authority (www.asa.org.uk).

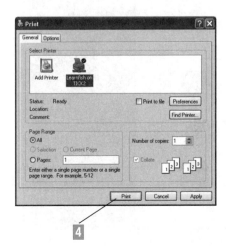

4.10.2 Checking Print Preview

1 Click on the File menu.

2 Click on Print Preview.

3 Use the arrow buttons to move through the pages.

4 Click on the Close button when you're finished.

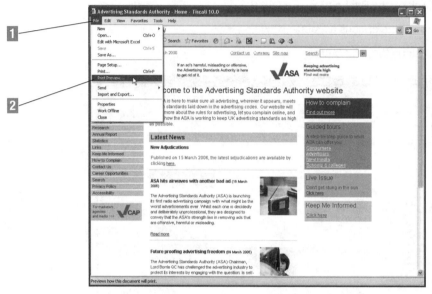

Copyright of the Advertising Standards Authority (www.asa.org.uk).

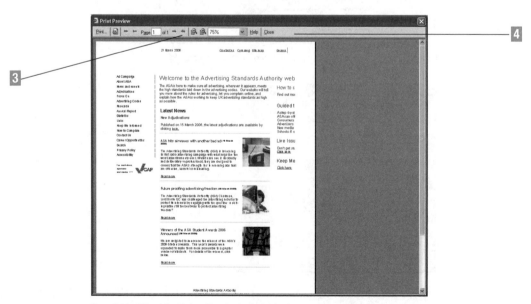

Copyright of the Advertising Standards Authority (www.asa.org.uk).

4.10.3 Printing a Single Frame

1 Select an item contained within the frame you want to print.

2 Click on the File menu.

3 Click on the Print option.

4 Click on the Options tab.

5 Make sure the **Only the selected frame option** is selected.

6 Click on the Print button.

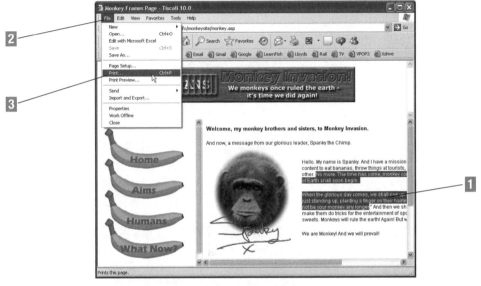

Screenshot provided courtesy of Happy (www.happy.co.uk).

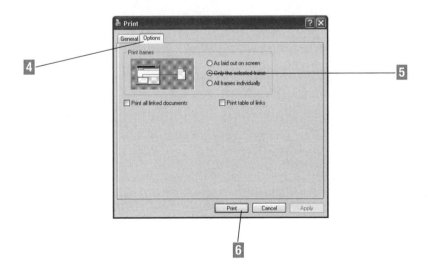

CHAPTER 5

Email Basics

5.1 Introduction

Email is the reason a lot of people get hooked up to the Internet in the first place. Electronic mail, to give it its full name, is one of the most simple, yet powerful, features of the Internet. It gives you the opportunity to contact anyone anywhere in the world within seconds, so long as they have an email address and a computer to check it on.

All you need to know is their address. Armed with that simple piece of knowledge, you can create a mail, send it to them, and know that it will arrive in their inbox within a matter of seconds. Who needs letters?!

There are dozens of different email programs out there and they're divided into two main types – web-based or PC-based. You may have heard of some popular web-based email programs, such as Hotmail, Yahoo! Mail and Google Mail. These have a great advantage, as they're not tied solely to your computer – you can access them from any Internet computer in the world.

PC-based email programs are those such as Microsoft's Outlook program. These will download your mail straight onto your PC when you open them. They're packed with features, so it's best to learn to use a program such as Outlook when you first start with email. You can then take your email skills onto the web if you decide you also need a web-based account.

5.2 The Outlook Screen and Starting Outlook

Microsoft Outlook is one of the programs contained within the Microsoft Office software package, and it's mainly used for sending email. However, that's not all it does. Outlook can also be used as a general planning tool as it includes calendar and journal features.

1 **Title bar**. Gives you the title of the program.

2 **Menu bar**. Gives you access to all the commands available in Outlook.

3 **Standard toolbar**. Click on any of the buttons for a quick way of performing that particular command.

4 **Outlook bar**. Lists the main areas of Microsoft Outlook. Click on any of these to go straight to that section.

5 **Inbox pane.** Lists all the emails you have received.

6 **Viewing pane.** Shows a preview of the selected email.

7 **Status bar.** Shows number of items in current folder and number unread.

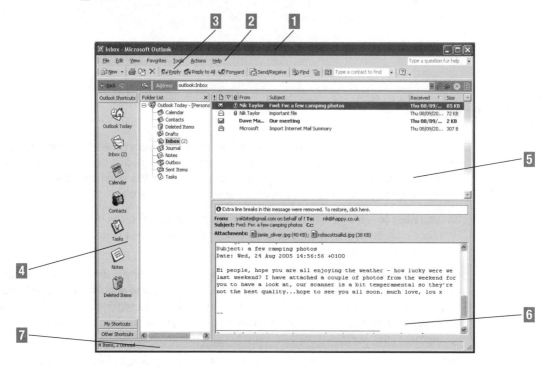

5.2.1 Starting Microsoft Outlook

1 Click on the Start button.

2 Click on the All Programs option.

3 Hold the mouse pointer over Microsoft Office.

4 Click on Microsoft Outlook.

5.2.2 Getting to the Inbox

1 Click on the Inbox icon on the Outlook bar.

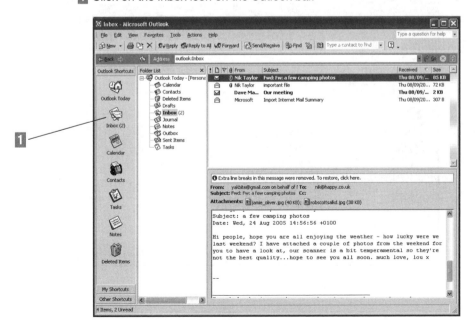

5.3 Creating an Email

Once you've got your email program up and running, you can get on with the important business of firing off a few emails to let everyone know you're online. Sending a simple email message takes hardly any time. All you need is the address of the person you want to mail and then you're ready to go.

There are plenty of further options you can take advantage of when sending emails. For instance, you can send the same message to lots of people at once, or send copies of the message to selected people.

5.3.1 Creating a New Email

1 Click on the Inbox icon on the Outlook bar.

2 Click on the New button.

3 Type in the address you wish to send to next to To, e.g. happy@happy.co.uk.

4 You can send a carbon copy of the email to anyone by typing their address in the Cc box.

5 Type in the subject next to Subject.

6 Type your message in the white space underneath.

7 Click on the Send button.

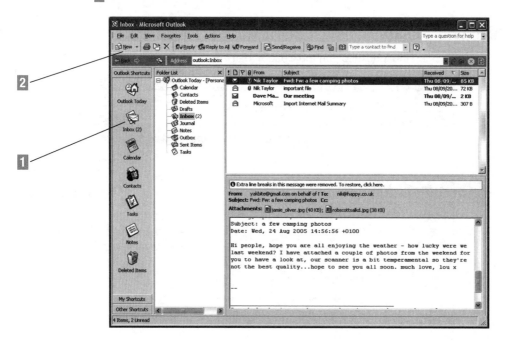

Sending emails to more than one person

You can send an email to more than one person. Separate the addresses with a semi-colon,e.g. happy@happy.co.uk; delirious@happy.co.uk.

Email etiquette

When you start writing emails, it's important to bear in mind a few of the conventions of this type of communication. If you write your email in capital letters, IT IS CONSIDERED SHOUTING, and is generally looked upon as being rather rude.

Some people like to send their friends files attached to their emails. However, attachments can take up a lot of space, and may take ages for your friend to download. It's a good idea to check with the intended recipient before you send them an attachment. They might not want it.

Every time you send an email, you'll see there is a space where you can type the subject of the message. By putting a relevant subject in the subject field, you can make sure the recipient knows what your email is about, without them having to wade through the whole thing straight away.

5.4 Email Options

There are a bunch of extra features you can use before you send off an email. For instance, if a message is extremely important (checking who's available to go for a drink after work, for instance), you can flag it up. When it arrives in the recipient's inbox, the flag will show them that the message is important and that they should respond.

Another useful feature is blind carbon copy. This enables you to add a person to the list of recipients, without them being visible to everyone else. For instance, you might send a message to Bob, Mary and Ismael, and then add Jerome as a blind carbon copy recipient. The mail will go to Jerome as well as the others, but Bob, Mary and Ismael will not be able to tell it was sent to him.

5.4.1 Flagging an Email Message

1 Create your message as normal.

2 Click the Flag icon.

3 Click the down arrow next to Flag to and choose the subject for the flag.

4 Click the down arrow next to Due by and choose the response date for the email.

5 Click OK.

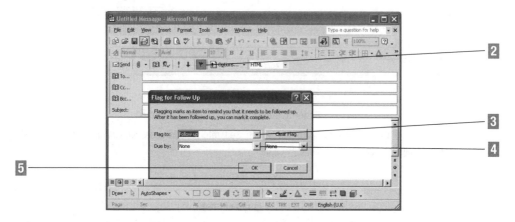

5.4.2 Sending a Blind Carbon Copy

1 Create your message as normal.

2 Click on the down arrow on the Options button.

3 Click on the Bcc field option (if it's not already ticked).

4 Type the address in the Bcc field.

5 Send the email as normal.

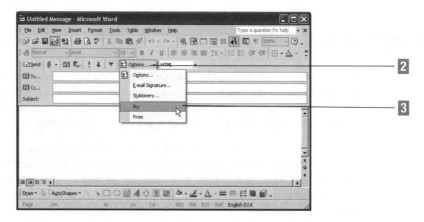

How email addresses work

Email addresses are usually made up of four parts. Let's use fredbloggs@johnsons.co.uk as an example.

The first part of an email address is the person's name or username. Following this is the @ symbol, which stands for **at**. So you have 'fred bloggs at'.

The next two parts of the address tell you where this person is to be found – so the email can get to them. Immediately after the @ sign, you'll see the location of the person's email account. This will either be a company, or an Internet Service Provider (ISP).

Our example email address then has two more elements at the end, separated by dots. The **.co** suffix shows you the email has come from a **co**mpany. The final part shows you the country from which the email has originated – in this case the UK.

5.5 Receiving and Reading Emails

Whoever said 'it's better to give than to receive' obviously never got round to getting an email account. There's nothing more guaranteed to brighten up a dull day at the office than having an interesting new email pop into your inbox.

Your email program will automatically check for incoming email every few minutes, but if you're feeling impatient you can hurry it along by clicking on the Send/Receive button.

Whenever you get a new message, you simply need to double click on it to read it. Messages you receive are stored in your Inbox. You'll easily be able to tell the difference between new messages and those you've already read. New messages will be listed in bold type and will have a closed envelope next to them. Those you have read will no longer be in bold type and the envelope icon will be opened. It's possible to make a read message look as though it hasn't been read, if you want to make sure you don't forget about it.

5.5.1 Receiving Email

1 Click on the Send/Receive button.

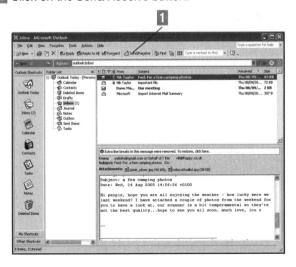

5.5.2 Reading New Mail

1 Click on the Inbox icon on the Outlook bar.

2 New messages will be listed in bold type and have a closed envelope icon next to them.

3 Double click the message to open it.

4 Close the message by clicking on the X at the top.

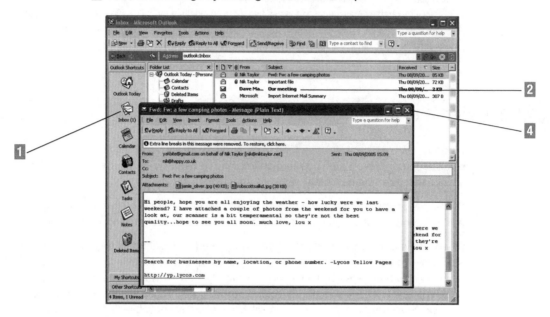

5.5.3 Marking Mail as Unread

1 Click on the message in the Inbox.

2 Click on Edit.

3 Click on Mark as Unread.

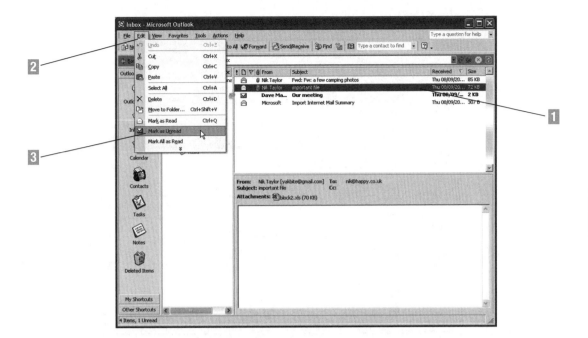

5.6 Replying and Forwarding Emails

Once you've read your new email, you're sure to want to say something back. You've got a couple of main options with a new mail: you can either reply to the original sender, or you can forward the whole message on to another person.

5.6.1 Forwarding a Message

1 Click on the Inbox icon on the Outlook bar.

2 Select the message you wish to forward.

3 Click Forward.

4 Enter the address you wish to forward to next to To.

5 Enter any text in the message area.

6 Send the message as normal.

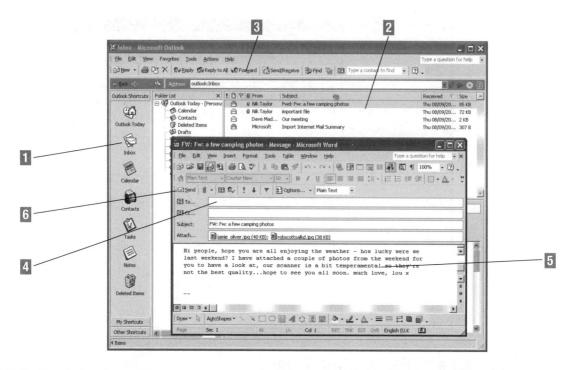

5.6.2 Replying to a Message

1 Select message to reply to.

2 Click Reply.

3 Type in your message.

4 Send the message as normal.

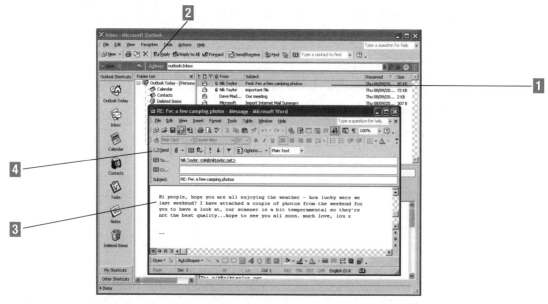

What is spam?

Spam is the general term for unsolicited email messages which are sent to you by people you've never met. It's called spam after the Monty Python sketch, where everything on the menu is served with spam!

These messages will often be adverts for websites, or they may contain improbable tales of how you can earn fabulous riches by sending some money to a foreign businessman. No matter what the content, if you receive an email you're not expecting, it's best ignored.

People often feel concerned that they are being personally targeted by spammers, but that's never the case. Spam senders normally buy huge lists of email addresses, and if yours happens to be on that list you will unfortunately receive some spam.

You can reduce your chances of receiving spam by only passing your email address to your friends and family, and avoiding typing it into online forms if possible. Most importantly, never reply to a spam email. All that will do is tell the sender your email address is active, so you'll get more messages.

If you receive unwanted emails from a reputable company, you can click on the Unsubscribe link at the bottom of the message. However, be cautious about doing this if you do not recognise the company or individual sending the message.

5.7 Replying Options

When you reply to an email you've received, you have a number of additional options. Particularly useful is the 'Reply to All' function. You can use this when you've received an email that's also been sent to several other people.

By choosing Reply to All, your response will be sent to all the people who received the original message, as well as the original sender. It's a particularly handy feature when having an email-based discussion with a group of friends or work colleagues.

Whenever you send any type of reply, the message you're replying to will be included in full at the bottom of the email. You might not want that to happen, so you can delete all or part of this quoted text before you send. Alternatively, you can change the settings of Outlook so it never includes the original message in replies.

5.7.1 Reply to All

1 Select the email you want to reply to.

2 Click on the Reply to All button.

3 Type in your message.

4 Send the email as usual.

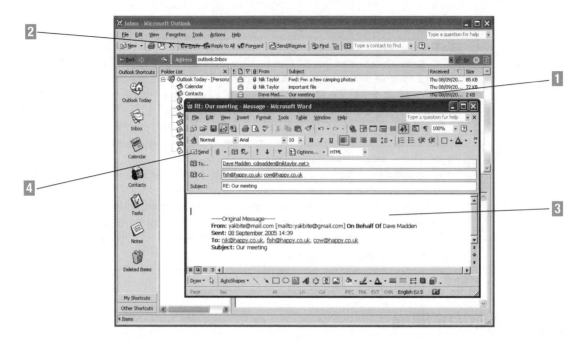

5.7.2 Setting Outlook to Not Include Message Text in Replies

1 Click Tools.

2 Click Options.

3 Click Preferences tab.

4 Click on the E-mail Options button.

5 Click the down arrow underneath When replying to a message.

6 Select Do not include original message.

7 Click OK.

8 Click OK.

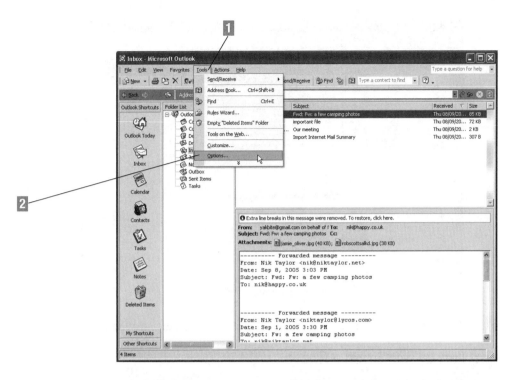

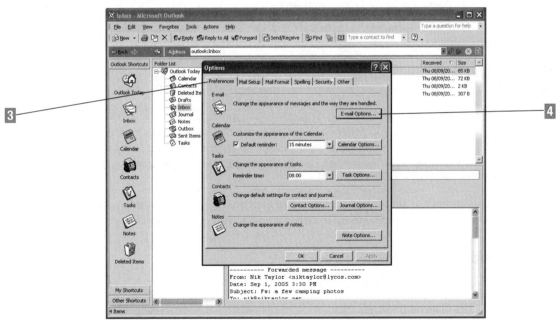

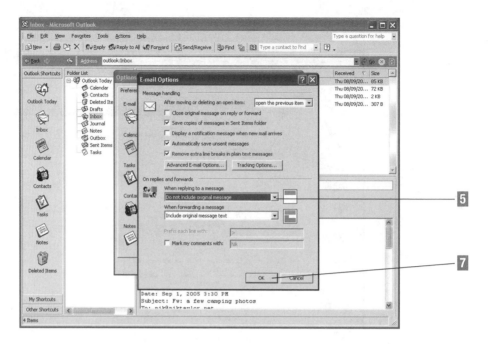

5.7.3 Deleting Part of Text From a Reply

1 Select the text you wish to delete.

2 Press Delete on the keyboard.

5.8 Attachments

Emails aren't just about sending text-based messages to all your friends. Whenever you send an email, you get the option to also attach files to it. This means you can send Word documents, Excel spreadsheets and any other type of file you fancy via the web. It also (and more often) means you can simply send some daft pictures round to all your colleagues.

It's easy to spot if you've received an attachment – just look out for a paperclip next to any new emails in your inbox. To open an attachment, just double click on the paper clip.

5.8.1 To Add an Attachment

1 Create a new email as usual.

2 Click on Insert.

3 Click on File.

4 Select the file you want to attach.

5 Click on the Insert button.

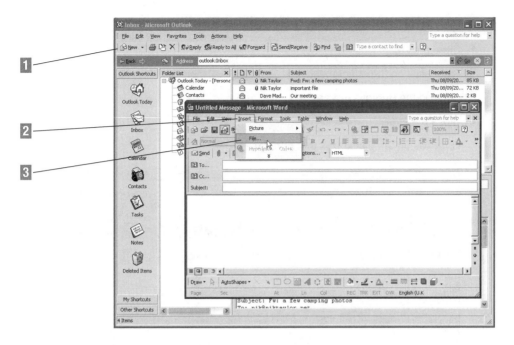

5.8.2 Saving a Received Attachment

1 Open the email.

2 Right click on the attachment.

3 Click on the Save As option.

4 Select a location in which to save the attachment.

5 Click on the Save button.

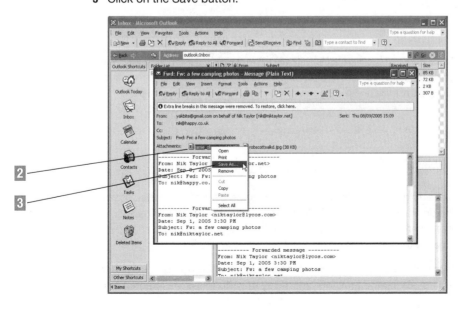

5.8.3 Removing an Attachment From a Received Email

1 Open the email.

2 Right click on the attachment.

3 Click on the Remove option.

4 Close the email.

5 Click Yes on the dialog box that appears.

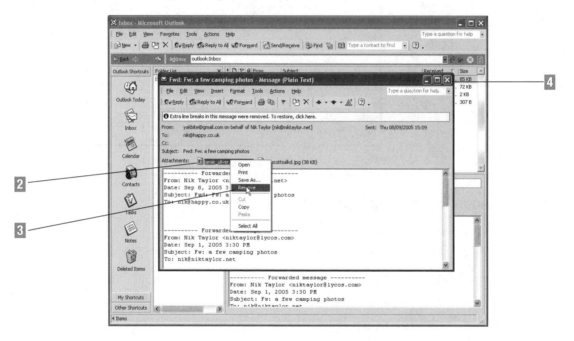

Look out!

Be careful when opening attachments you have received, as this is the easiest way to infect your computer with a virus (see next section). A simple rule of thumb is to never open an attachment unless it's one you're expecting – even if it comes from someone you know.

5.9 Viruses

Before you get carried away with all the excitement of email attachments, let's look at one of the downsides. The vast majority of the attachments you'll receive will cause you no problems at all. However, very, very occasionally you might receive an attachment that is infected with a virus.

A virus is a malicious computer program which is designed to spread from computer to computer. By far the most common way they do this is via infected email attachments. If you receive one of these and open it, your PC will become infected. That's bad news, as it's fairly likely your PC will be damaged in some way. The good news is that, although there are plenty of viruses out there, so long as you're reasonably cautious you're unlikely to be affected by them.

If you receive an email you were not expecting with an attachment, you should be wary – and you certainly shouldn't open it. Email viruses cannot be activated until you open an infected attachment, so if you simply delete the email straight away, you will be perfectly safe. If the email has come from a friend, get in touch with them to check it is safe to open before doing so. Viruses can hijack email accounts and use them to spread themselves, so if a friend's machine has been infected, their email account may be spreading the virus without their knowledge.

5

Useful anti-virus sites

AVG Anti-Virus
www.grisoft.com

Symantec
www.symantec.com

Sophos
www.sophos.com

Trend Micro
www.trendmicro.com

McAfee
www.mcafee.com

Panda Software
www.pandasoftware.com

5.9.1 Checking for Virus Hoaxes

Viruses are often a source of panic among computer users. This has led to the proliferation of virus hoaxes, which are sent by email. There's one very easy way to tell if you have received a hoaxed virus alert. Aside from all the capital letters and exclamation marks, you'll see somewhere a phrase along the lines of 'email this message to all your friends straight away!!!'

This is a clear giveaway that the message you have received is a hoax. A genuine virus alert will never implore you to forward it on to your entire address book. You can check whether the virus warning is genuine by visiting an anti-virus website.

1 Go to the web address www.sophos.com.

2 Click on the security information link.

3 Click on the Hoaxes link.

4 Click on the first letter of the virus name mentioned in the email.

5 Click on the name of the virus mentioned.

6 If the hoax is not listed, repeat the above steps in the Threat analyses section to see if you are being warned about a real virus.

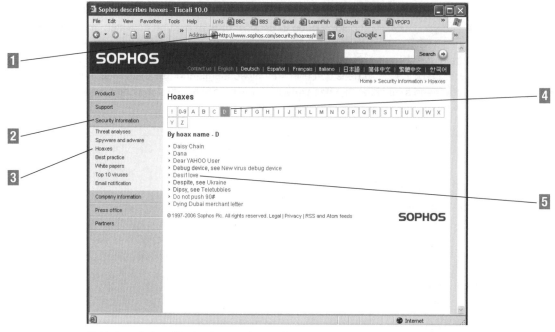

By kind permission of Sophos (www.sophos.com).

5.10 Organising Email

Well-connected social animal that you are, it will be just a few hours before your email inbox is bursting at the seams with thousands of messages, which will leave you with something of a conundrum – how to find the email you want from among the melee.

The simplest way to dig up an email is to sort them by type. For instance, by clicking on the From header, you can instantly sort all the emails by the name of their sender.

You can also keep your emails neatly organised by creating new folders and moving your messages into them.

5.10.1 The Folder List

Folders are used in Outlook to organise your emails. The Inbox is one folder, and there are folders for emails you have sent, deleted, and so on. To show the folder list...

1 Click on the View menu.

2 Click on Folder list.

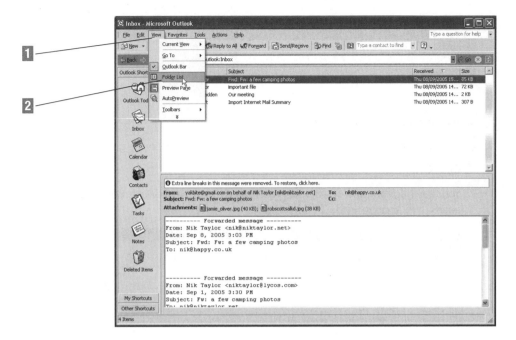

5.10.2 Switching Between Folders

1 Click on the folder name you want to view.

2 Click on the plus symbol to open a folder and view the sub-folders within.

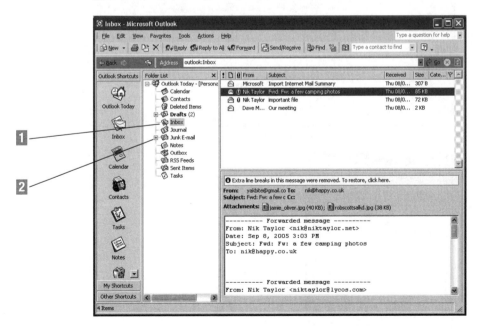

5.10.3 Creating a New Folder

⬛ Click File.

⬛ Click New.

⬛ Click Folder.

⬛ Type in a name for your folder.

⬛ Click on the folder which will 'hold' the folder you are creating, e.g. Inbox.

⬛ Click OK.

7 You may be prompted on whether you wish to create a shortcut. Click Yes if you wish a shortcut to appear on the Outlook Bar.

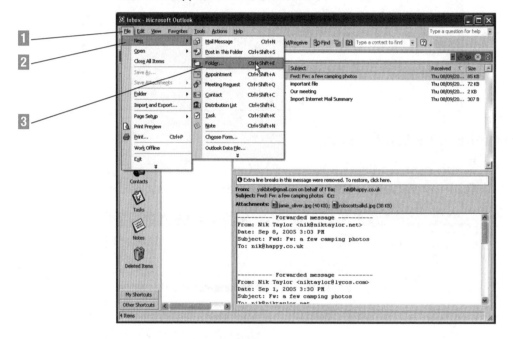

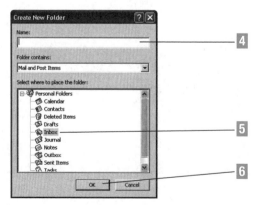

5.10.4 Moving an Email to a New Folder

1 Click on the email you wish to move.

2 Click Edit.

3 Click Move to Folder.

4 Click on the folder you wish to move it to.

5 Click OK.

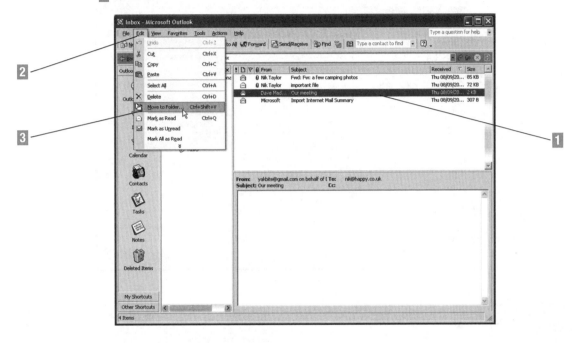

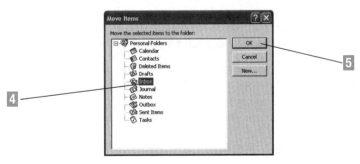

5.10.5 Sorting Emails by Type

1 Go to the folder you wish to sort.

2 Click on the grey bar you want to sort by (e.g. subject).

3 Click on the grey bar again to sort in reverse order.

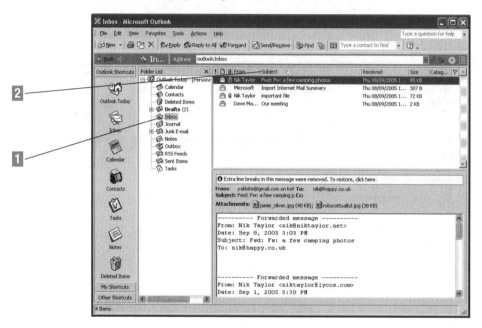

5.11 Creating Contacts

Chuck away your little black book – you can store all the details of friends and colleagues in Outlook's Contacts section. The main purpose of this feature is to enable you to store email addresses, so you don't need to type them in full each time you send a message.

In addition, you can store information such as postal addresses and phone numbers. Click on the Contacts option on the navigation pane to get to this area.

5.11.1 Creating a New Contact

1 Click on the Contacts icon on the Outlook bar.

2 Click on the New button.

3 Fill in the details.

4 Click on Save and Close.

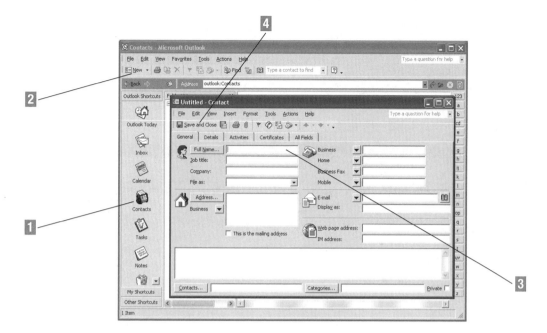

5.11.2 Adding a Contact from a Received Email

1 Right click on an email address on an email.

2 Click on Add to Contacts.

3 Fill in extra details.

4 Click on Save and Close.

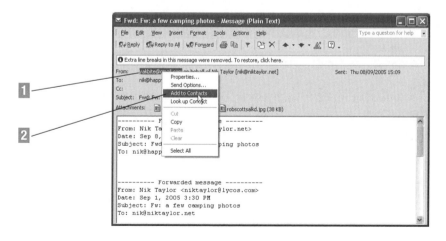

5.11.3 Editing a Contact

1 Double click on a contact to open it.

2 Make changes.

3 Click on Save and Close.

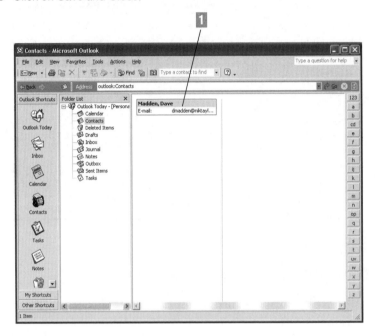

5.11.4 Deleting a Contact

1 Click on the contact.

2 Press the Delete key.

5.11.5 Using Contacts

1 Open a new email.

2 Click on the To button.

3 Click on the name from the list.

4 Click on the OK button.

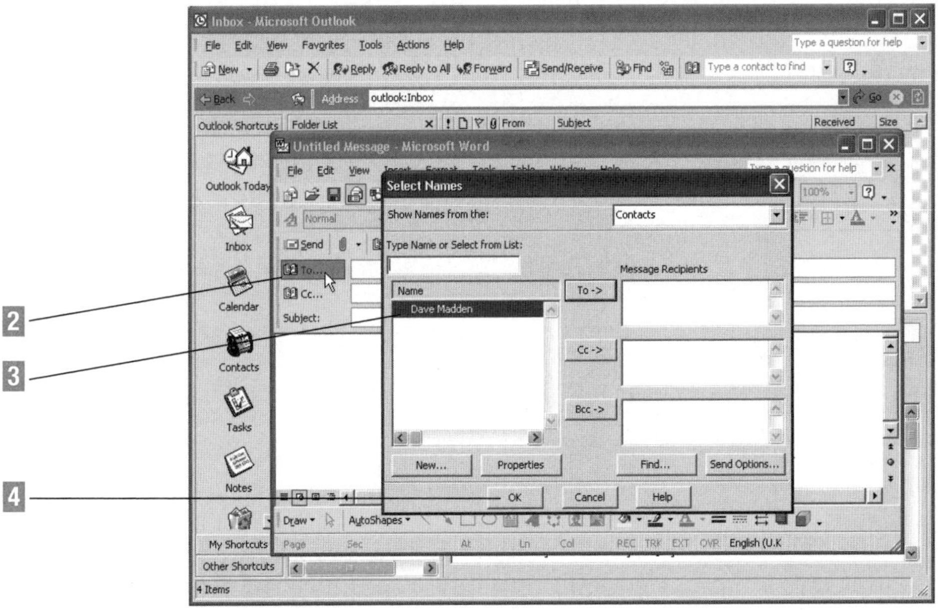
2
3
4
Inbox - Microsoft Outlook
Untitled Message - Microsoft Word
Select Names
Show Names from the:
Contacts
Type Name or Select from List:
Message Recipients
Name
Dave Madden
To ->
Cc ->
Bcc ->
New...
Properties
Find...
Send Options...
OK
Cancel
Help

CHAPTER 6

Using Forms

6.1 Introduction

Filling in forms isn't much fun, but if you want to make full use of the Internet you're going to need to know how to complete them online.

Pretty much every site that you can interact with (e.g. message boards, web-based email sites, online shops and so on) require you to first register – and that means you need to fill in a form.

Forms can also be used to enable you to interact with a website. For instance, if you want to find out what time a train leaves from your local station, you can go to a train timetable site. When you load the site, you'll need to fill in a form giving the details of the journey you want to make.

Online form filling isn't normally a particularly time-consuming process. For instance, if you're registering for a site you just need to submit a few personal details, such as your name, date of birth and email address. Once you've done this, you'll be given your own personal account with which you can access the pages of the site.

The main way of providing these details to a website is to simply type them into boxes known as 'fields'. However, you'll also come across a range of other ways to fill in forms, using drop-down menus, radio buttons, checkboxes and more.

6.2 Filling in Online Forms

You'll be asked for your details all the time when online. A large amount of sites require you to register before you can use all of the available functions, e.g. online shops, banks, email accounts and so on. There are several different ways to enter your details into an online form. Here are the main ones:

- **Fields**. These are simply empty boxes into which you type the requested detail.

- **Drop-down menus**. These contain a pre-defined list of options. Click on the menu, then click on the option you want.

- **Radio buttons**. A list of options, with a button next to each. You can click on one button to select it. Click on another button and the previously selected button will become deselected. Named after the old-fashioned radios where you pushed a button to move to a particular station.

- **Checkboxes**. An option with a box next to it. Click on the box and it will fill with a tick, to show it is selected. Click on it again to deselect it.

6.2.1 Completing Fields

1 Click inside the field so you can see the text insertion point flashing.

2 Type in the requested detail.

3 Click into the next field to continue adding data.

Moving from one field to another

When you've finished typing into a field, press the Tab key on your keyboard to move to the next. This is the key directly above the Caps Lock key on the left of the keyboard. To move back to the previous field, hold down the Shift key and press Tab.

6.2.2 Editing Fields

1 Click inside the field you've typed in.

2 Change the existing text.

3 Click outside the field.

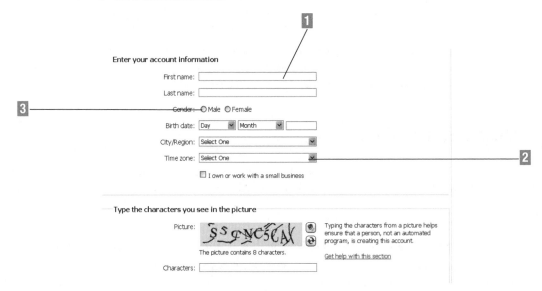

Screenshot from Yahoo! (www.yahoo.co.uk).

6.2.3 Using Drop-down Menus

1 Click on the down-pointing arrow.

2 Scroll down the list if necessary.

3 Click on the desired option.

6.2.4 Using Checkboxes

1 Click on the box so a tick (or other mark) appears.

2 Click on the box again to deselect the option.

Checkboxes might not be box-shaped!

These parts of forms are just called checkboxes for ease of use. They could just as easily be circles, rather than boxes. The main thing is, they all work in the same way. You can select as many boxes as you like without having to deselect any.

6.2.5 Using Radio Buttons

1 Click on the button next to the option you want to select.

2 Click on a different button if you want to change the option (the previous option will be deselected).

6.2.6 Submitting Data

1 Click on the button at the bottom of the form. This will usually have the word 'Submit' or 'Enter' on it.

Error messages

If you type in any of the required data wrongly, you'll see an error message when you click the Submit button. Click OK once you've read the message, and correct the error.

Filling in forms automatically

There are lots of programs out there that can fill in forms for you automatically. One such example is the Google toolbar (http://toolbar.google.com/). Download this and it will appear among your toolbars at the top of your browser window. Among the features of this toolbar is AutoFill. Once you've set up this feature, one click of the AutoFill button will instantly add all your details to a form.

6.3 Filling in a Form on Yahoo! Mail

There are several different features you need to be able to use in order to fill in an online form. The simplest way to understand how these work is to go through the process yourself. Follow the instructions in this section to fill in a form signing you up for a Yahoo! Mail account. Once you've completed the process, you'll have your own Yahoo! Mail email address which you can use if you wish. The form you need to fill in contains all the features you'll find on any other forms on the Internet.

6.3.1 Accessing the Form

1 Load the Yahoo! site (http://uk.yahoo.com) in your browser.

2 Click on the Mail icon at the top of the page.

3 Click on the Try It Now button.

Screenshot from Yahoo! (www.yahoo.co.uk).

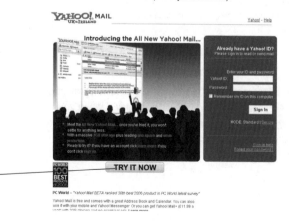

Screenshot from Yahoo! (www.yahoo.co.uk).

6.3.2 Filling in the Form

1 These are text boxes. Click into any of these and type in the details requested.

2 These are drop-down menus. Click on top of these, then click on the option you want.

3 Type in the Yahoo! ID you want here. This will form the beginning part of your email address.

4 You can find out if this ID has already been taken by clicking on the Check Availability of This ID button.

5 If the ID is available, click on the Continue… button. Otherwise, type another ID into the Try another Yahoo! ID box, then click on the Check Availability of This ID button.

6 This is a checkbox. Click here if you want to receive Yahoo! promotional emails. Click it again to deselect.

7 Type the characters you see in the large box into this box.

8 Click on the I Agree button to submit your form.

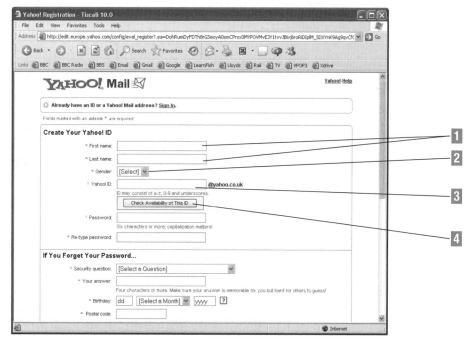

Screenshot from Yahoo! (www.yahoo.co.uk).

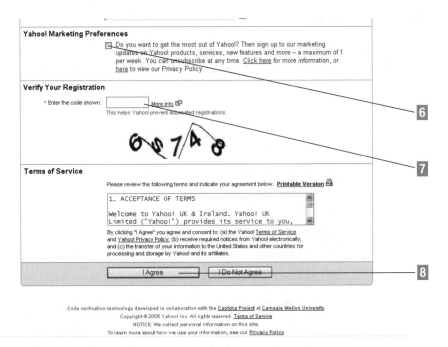

Yahoo! Marketing Preferences

☐ Do you want to get the most out of Yahoo!? Then sign up to our marketing updates on Yahoo! products, services, new features and more – a maximum of 1 per week. You can unsubscribe at any time. Click here for more information, or here to view our Privacy Policy.

Verify Your Registration

* Enter the code shown: [   ] More info 🖼

This helps Yahoo! prevent automated registrations.

6 ꜱ 7 4 8

Terms of Service

Please review the following terms and indicate your agreement below. **Printable Version** 🖨

1. ACCEPTANCE OF TERMS

Welcome to Yahoo! UK & Ireland. Yahoo! UK Limited ("Yahoo!") provides its service to you,

By clicking "I Agree" you agree and consent to: (a) the Yahoo! Terms of Service and Yahoo! Privacy Policy; (b) receive required notices from Yahoo! electronically; and (c) the transfer of your information to the United States and other countries for processing and storage by Yahoo! and its affiliates.

[I Agree]   [I Do Not Agree]

6
7
8

Code verification technology developed in collaboration with the Captcha Project at Carnegie Mellon University.
Copyright © 2005 Yahoo! Inc. All rights reserved. Terms of Service
NOTICE: We collect personal information on this site.
To learn more about how we use your information, see our Privacy Policy

Screenshot from Yahoo! (www.yahoo.co.uk).

What is the verification for?

As part of the form you fill in to get a Yahoo! email address, you're asked to type in some strange looking characters. This is to ensure you are a real person applying for an account and not a computer. It prevents people from signing up automatically for hundreds of accounts using computer software.

CHAPTER 7

Staying Safe Online

7.1 Introduction

Going online for the first time can be an unsettling experience. The media is full of scare stories of unwitting surfers getting ripped off, having their identities stolen, their credit card accounts maxed out and so on.

Now, we're not going to tell you such risks don't exist, and it would be a very bad idea to completely disregard the possibility of online fraud. However, if you follow some simple pointers, you will have no problem staying safe on the Internet.

For a start, it's a good idea to keep up a healthy level of cynicism when online. The Net is full of adverts offering instant riches or high-value items for free. Such adverts are persuasively written and it's easy to be tempted to take a closer look. The best thing to do is to simply think, 'Does this seem too good to be true'? If it does, then it probably is!

You'll get plenty of these type of adverts through your email. Advertisers can get hold of your email address when they buy huge mailing lists, and they'll then send you unwanted adverts trying to get you to shop with them. More worryingly, you may also receive emails from con-artists, trying to get you to share details such as your log-in for online banking. These are easily spotted, however, once you know what you're looking for.

One of the most useful features of going online is the chance to shop from your own home. Many people are put off from doing this because they've heard stories about it being unsafe. This is a shame, because as long as you keep an eye out for a few key things, you can guarantee your details will be safe when you shop online.

If you're concerned about what sites other members of your family are able to access, you can invest in some protection software that will enable you to restrict certain types of site from being accessible on your computer.

7.2 Avoiding Misleading Information

The old adage 'don't believe everything you read' holds just as true for the Internet as for anywhere else. Although the so-called dangers of the Internet are often over-exaggerated in the press and other media, it certainly pays to be cautious when online.

Anyone can create a website about anything they like – so don't take everything you read on the Internet as gospel. If the page you're reading comes from a major company you know and trust, you should be a lot more confident about its content than if you're reading advice from someone's personal web pages, for instance.

One of the areas of the Internet in which you'll most commonly find misleading information is advertising. The relevant authorities, such as the Advertising Standards Authority (ASA), can clear up any misleading adverts published by UK-based companies. However, since the Net is a global medium, there are tons of adverts online which are not covered by the same laws.

Adverts you'll typically come across will often be of the 'too good to be true' type that offer to make you potloads of cash for very little effort. For example, you may see an advert that claims to offer a home-working opportunity through which you can make thousands of pounds per month for only a few hours' work. Notably, the advert won't go into any detail about what work is involved. The important thing to remember about these incredible-sounding deals is that if they really worked, everyone would be doing them.

7.2.1 Reporting Misleading Adverts

1 Load the ASA site (www.asa.org.uk) in your browser.

2 Click on the How to Complain link on the left.

3 Click on the online complaints form link.

4 Fill in the form.

5 Click on the Submit button.

Copyright of the Advertising Standards Authority (www.asa.org.uk).

Copyright of the Advertising Standards Authority (www.asa.org.uk).

Is this the right site to use?

The ASA only deals with complaints about certain types of advertisement. Click on the 'check we're the right people to complain to' link in the How to Complain section to make sure your complaint is going to the right people. There's advice here on where to direct your complaint otherwise.

7.3 Dodgy Emails

Much of the misleading advertising you'll see on the Internet will come via your email inbox. An ever-present problem on the Internet is the presence of rip-off merchants who will try to scam you via email. Such scams are annoying – but very easily spotted.

Among the most well-known of these is 419 fraud. These scams typically originate from Nigeria – the name 419 fraud comes from the section of the Nigerian penal code that deals with these cons.

Potential victims receive an email containing an outlandish story about a businessman who needs to transfer millions of dollars out of his country. The recipient has, apparently, been chosen especially to help, and will receive a hefty cut of the money for their assistance. However, that assistance involves first sending some money the businessman's way...

Never respond to emails such as this. The very fact that it's come from someone you've never met should set alarm bells ringing straight away. The fact that they want money should see you reaching for the delete key.

Another scam you should be aware of is known as phishing. This is where fraudsters send out emails, posing as legitimate sites. For example, a message may appear in your Inbox, claiming to be from your bank. It will go something along the lines of:

Dear Sir/Madam,

We have noticed a problem with your account. Your monies will be frozen until you click on this link and log on to our site... etc.

If you click on the link and fill in your details, the scammers will have access to your accounts. A reputable company will never ask you to send sensitive details via email, and will never ask you to click through a link in an email in this way. If a company you deal with sends you an email you're unsure about, just give them a ring to double-check its veracity.

Be aware of these scams, but don't worry too much about them. If you receive an email you're worried about, there are plenty of sites you can visit to check whether it's a known scam.

7.3.1 Checking for Existing Phishing Emails

1 Load up the Anti-Phishing Working Group site (www.antiphishing.org) in your browser.

2 Click on the Phishing Archive link.

3 Scroll through the list to check for the email you've received.

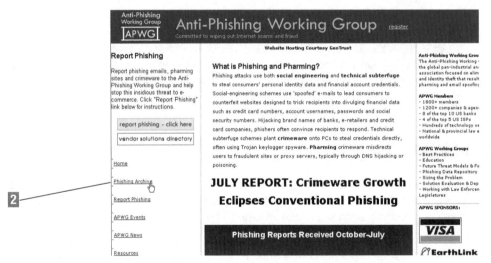

By kind permission of the Anti-Phishing Working Group (www.antiphishing.org).

Not all phishing emails are listed here!

This site can be a useful resource, but it's impossible for it to list all the phishing scams out there. If you're unsure about any email you've received from a company you have dealings with, make telephone contact to check whether it is truthful.

7.4 | Computer Misuse

Computers are an important part of modern life, but there is the potential to misuse them. There are a variety of things that could constitute computer misuse, and some of these actions are illegal.

The law regarding computers in the UK is still in its infancy. However, some of the computer-based actions that are against the law in the UK are:

1 Hacking into websites

2 Creating or deliberately transmitting viruses

3 Viewing or storing illegal pornography

4 Creating a criminally racist site

But you should remember that misuse cannot simply be defined by whether something is legal or not. For example, most Internet cafes will have a policy which their customers are expected to follow. If you break this policy, that would also be considered as misuse.

However, you're most likely to find a policy on proper Internet use when you're at work. Although it might feel like 'your' computer – those bods in the tecnical department will never tire of telling you that it actually belongs to 'the company'. Therefore, there may be lots of things that you're not allowed to do with the PC.

For instance, you may be banned from using file-sharing programs, which enable people to share files from their computers. These are a very easy way to pick up viruses, and they're also used for illegal activities such as sharing copyrighted material. You may also be banned from using Internet chat sites, or downloading programs from the web.

If you want to put such restrictions in place on your own computer, you can download special programs that can monitor which sites are being visited, and can be set up to make it impossible to access particular sites. Similar programs can also compile a log of all activity that takes place on your computer.

7.4.1 Finding Parental Control Programs

1 Go to a search engine such as Google (www.google.co.uk).

2 Run a search for 'parental control'.

3 Click on one of the links to suitable programs that will appear.

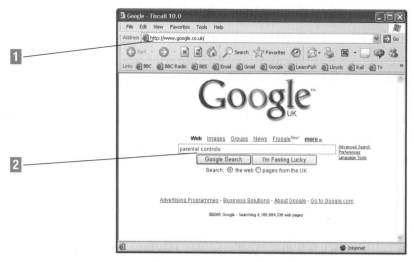

By kind permission of Google (www.google.co.uk).

Some popular parental control programs

CyberPatrol – www.cyberpatrol.com

NetNanny – www.netnanny.com

Cybersitter – www.cybersitter.com

7.5 Secure Shopping

One of the great perks of using the Internet is being able to do all your shopping without going anywhere near a busy high street.

However, many people are put off shopping online because of concerns about safety. This needn't be an issue, however, so long as the site you're shopping on is secure. If the shopping site you use is secure, that means all the payment information you submit is encrypted – making it impossible for any potential thiefs to intercept.

If you're using a secure site, you will see a locked padlock appear in the status bar at the bottom of your browser window. Additionally, the web address in the address bar will begin 'https', instead of just http. You may also have a message appear as you load up the secure page. These changes will only show up on a secure site once you have clicked through to the payment page.

If someone defrauds your card to shop online, you can cancel the payment and can claim a full refund from your card issuer. In addition, if you've made a purchase of more than £100 using a credit (not debit) card, you will also be covered for some other eventualities. Using your credit card can be handy if you want to make a claim against the seller for not supplying your order, or for faulty goods.

In these instances, you may be covered by the credit card. You can get further peace of mind by looking out for shops that are affiliated to safe shopping schemes. One such scheme is the Government-run TrustUK.

7.5.1 Spotting Secure Shops

1 The address will begin with https.

2 There will be a closed padlock at the bottom of the screen.

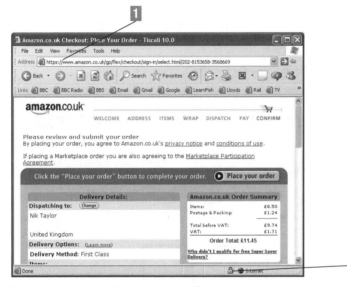

Screenshot from Amazon (www.amazon.co.uk).

Safe shopping schemes

TrustUK – www.trustuk.org.uk

Safebuy – www.safebuy.org.uk

VeriSign – www.verisign.com

7.6 Protecting your Details

It may surprise you to know this, but your personal details are probably stored in the files of at least ten companies. Your bank, your place of work, people you have bought goods from, your council and others will all have kept hold of some of your details. Online shops will often store details too, such as your name, address and card details.

When you buy from an online company, you're entitled to know whether this is the case. Reputable companies are likely to provide a link to a privacy statement, where they will explain what they do with information held on you. If the company stores your payment details, it will also explain how secure those details are.

Companies will often pass your details on to other businesses who may want to contact you with offers they think you will be interested in. If you don't want this to happen, you can click on an opt-out box during the purchase process.

7.6.1 Keeping your Details Private

All websites will have slightly different privacy policies, but they all follow a similar style. Companies are not allowed to pass on your details if you don't want them to, so look out for the opt-out sections on any sites you sign up for.

1 Tick this box if you want to receive promotional emails.

2 Click on this link to view the site's Terms of Service.

3 Click on this link to view the site's Privacy Policy.

4 Click on this button to show you agree with the Terms of Service and Privacy Policy.

Screenshot from Yahoo! (www.yahoo.co.uk).

7.7 Checking your Rights

Many of your rights when buying online from a UK-based company are the same as when you buy from a shop.

You also benfit from some additional rights, because you are buying from distance.

Online stores must offer a 'cooling off' period, during which you can cancel your order without any reason and get a full refund. If you have purchased goods, this period extends up to seven days after you have received your order. If the order isn't delivered by the date you agreed, you can claim a full refund. If you didn't agree a date, you can get a full refund if the order isn't fulfilled within 30 days.

You also have other rights when shopping on the Internet, such as the right to:

- clear information about the goods or services offered before you buy

- written confirmation of this information after you have made your purchase

There are several instances in which the additional rights do not apply. Online auctions are not included, for example. Your rights are also different if the goods you've ordered are perishable – such as food or fresh flowers.

7.7.1 Check Your Rights with the Office of Fair Trading

1 Load the Office of Fair Trading site (www.oft.gov.uk) in your browser.

2 Click on the Consumer Information link.

3 Click on the Online Shopping link and read through the information.

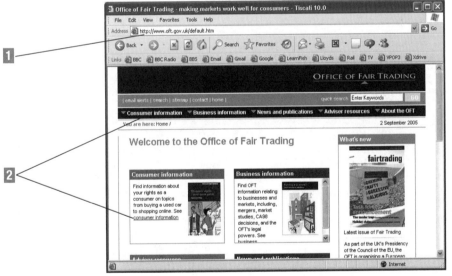

By kind permission of the Office of Fair Trading (www.oft.gov.uk).

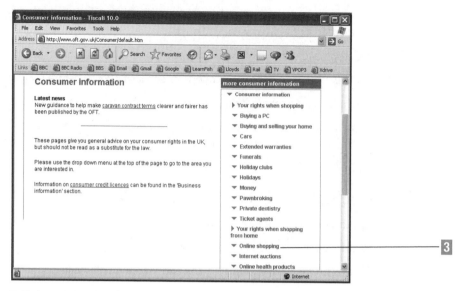

By kind permission of the Office of Fair Trading (www.oft.gov.uk).

CHAPTER 8

Search Engines

8.1 Introduction

The World Wide Web is a huge, sprawling place. No-one knows how many web pages there are out there, but the number is comfortably over three billion. Such gargantuan figures pose an obvious problem. How on earth are you supposed to find your way around?

The answer lies in a type of website known as a search engine. These clever little programs scour the Internet, compiling a list of all the sites they find on the way. You can then run a search via one of these sites to find the pages you want.

Running a search is simple. You just type in a few words that describe the type of page you're looking for, then hit the 'search' button. Within a second or so, the search engine will pop up a list of all the sites that match your requirements. All you need to do then is click on the link for the site that looks most like what you're after.

Often, such a basic search will come up with an enormous number of results. The easiest way to cut this down to a more manageable number is to make your search more specific using the advanced search features. These enable you to search only for sites within a particular country, or to search for exact phrases on a site.

Even more specific are the specialist search engines. These sites search the web for only particular types of content – for instance, pictures, sound files, or sites on a set subject.

8.2 Using Google

There are literally thousands of different search engines on the Internet, but one towers above them all – the ubiquitous Google. This mammothly popular website has even made inroads into the English language as a verb. Ask someone to find you something on the Net and don't be surprised if they reply, 'OK, I'll just go and Google it', instead of, 'I'll just go and search for it'.

The popularity of the site is well founded – it's the very model of simplicity. There is very little to see on the Google website, but what's there is supremely useful.

8.2.1 Running a Basic Search

1 Load the site in your browser (www.google.co.uk).

2 Type keywords describing what you're looking for into the search box.

3 Click on the relevant radio button ('the web' to search the whole of the Internet, 'pages from the UK' to search only UK-specific content).

4 Click on the Google Search button.

5 Click on the title of the search result you want to look at.

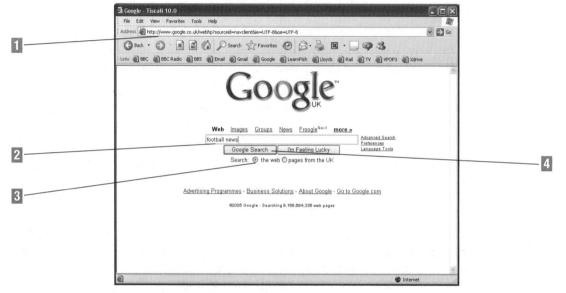

By kind permission of Google (www.google.co.uk).

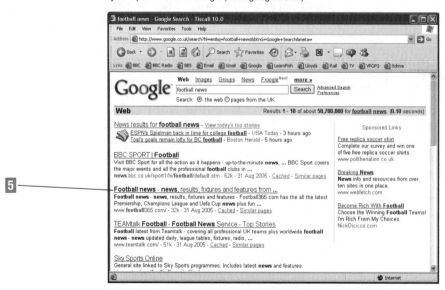

By kind permission of Google (www.google.co.uk).

What's 'I'm Feeling Lucky'?

Next to the 'Google Search' button is the 'I'm Feeling Lucky' button. Click this and you'll go straight to the first search result found for your particular search.

Running other types of search

You can use the links above the search window to specify the type of content you want to find. For example, if you want to find a picture of your favourite cricketer, click on the Images link. You can now make a search using Google Image Search – which looks only for pictures.

Web – click here to search the whole web

Images – click here to search for pictures

Groups – click here to search through newsgroup postings

News – click here to search only through news stories

Froogle – click here to search for the lowest price on a product

Searching for a specific phrase

To run a search for a specific phrase (such as a book title) you can enclose the search terms in speech marks like this: 'Bleak House'.

8.3 Using Google's Advanced Search

The front page of Google is kept deliberately simple, but there are stacks more features you can use to make your web searching more accurate. On the home page, click on the Advanced Search link to access these extra features.

It's useful to use the Advanced Search when you're looking for something very specific and don't want to wade through thousands of results. By tweaking the extra options, you can adjust Google so, for example, it only looks for recently changed sites, or only looks for your search terms in the title of a page.

8.3.1 Advanced Search

1 Use the Find Results section to specify the keywords you want Google to search for. Type keywords into any or all of the four fields here.

2 Click on the drop-down menu and select which Language you want the results to be returned in.

3 Use the File format drop-down menus to find or ignore results, in particular file formats.

4 Use the Date drop-down menu to find results within a set time-frame.

5 Click on the Occurrences drop-down menu to find where the keywords should be found (in title, in URL etc.)

6 Use the Domain section to limit the search to only certain domains (e.g. educational websites).

7 Click on the button to specify whether the search should be filtered to exclude adult content.

8 Click on the Google Search button.

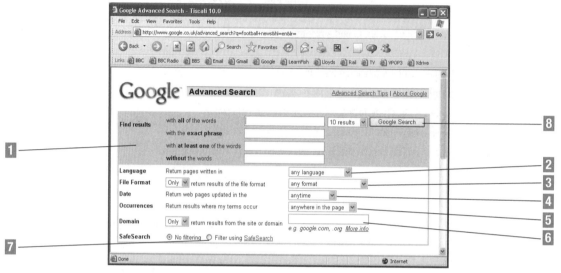

By kind permission of Google (www.google.co.uk).

Search for similar sites

At the bottom of the Google Advanced Search page are two boxes you can use to search for related sites. Type a website address into either of the boxes, then click on the Search button. Use the 'Similar' box to find sites that are similar to the one you've specified. Use the 'Links' box to find sites that link to the one you've specified.

8.4 Using Lycos

Of course, there's more to searching on the Internet than just using Google. It's a good idea to have a varied list of search engines you can use, as each offers varous benefits. Lycos is another of the big names on the searching scene, but it takes a very different approach to Google.

Instead of bare-bones simplicity, Lycos opts for an all-singing, all-dancing page that offers links for everything from online dating to the latest weather forecast. In the middle of it all is the search window.

8.4.1 Running a Basic Search

1 Load the site in your browser (www.lycos.co.uk).

2 Type your search keywords into the search box.

3 Click on the radio button that specifies the type of search you want to make.

4 Click on the Search button.

5 Click on the link of the search result you want.

Screenshot from Lycos (www.lycos.co.uk).

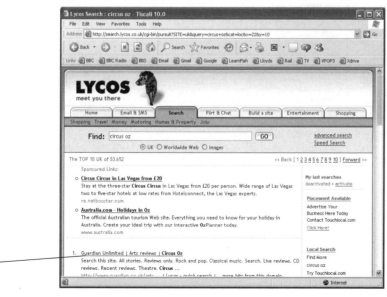

Screenshot from Lycos (www.lycos.co.uk).

8.4.2 Running an Advanced Search

1 Load the site in your browser (www.lycos.co.uk).

2 Click on the Advanced Search link.

3 Type keywords into any or all of the four boxes in the 'Please look for' section.

4 Click on the relevant 'Search Area' button to specify what you want to search for.

5 Click on the Target Area boxes to select which parts of the site you want to search.

6 Click on the File Format boxes to select what type of files you want to search for.

7 Use the Domain section to limit the search to only certain domains (e.g. educational websites).

8 Click on the relevant button in the Family Filter section to choose whether you want your results filtered.

9 Click on the Go button.

Screenshot from Lycos (www.lycos.co.uk).

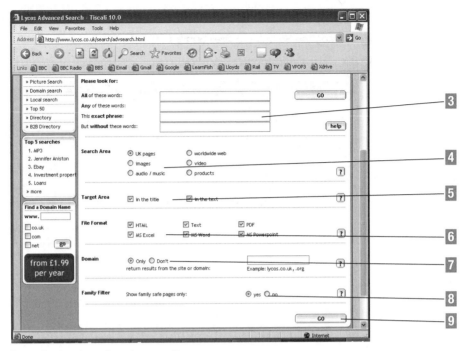

Screenshot from Lycos (www.lycos.co.uk).

Using tick-boxes

The Lycos Advanced Search page includes lots of what's known as tick-boxes. These are used to select options. If you want the option to be selected, make sure the box is ticked. If not, make sure it is unticked. You can toggle between the two by clicking on top of the box.

8.5 Using Yahoo!

Another famous and popular search engine is Yahoo! Wherever you go on Yahoo! you will be assailed by exclamation marks, but apart from that it's a fairly impressive search engine. There are actually two main search sites run by Yahoo!, one of which looks a bit like Google, the other of which is a bit like Lycos. For sheer searching power and simplicity of use, the Google-alike at http://uk.search.yahoo.com is the better bet.

8.5.1 Running a Basic Search

1 Load the site at http://uk.search.yahoo.com.

2 Click on the link above the search box that describes what you want to search for.

3 Click the radio button below the Search the Web that describes the country in which you wish to search.

4 Type some keywords into the search box.

5 Click on the Search the Web button.

6 Click on the title of the search result you want to view.

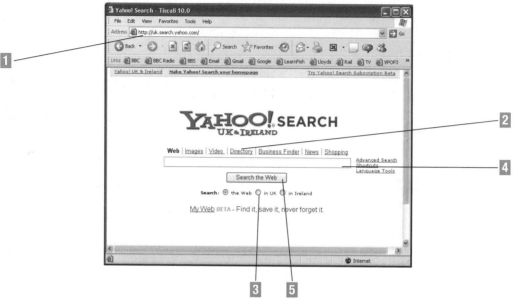

Screenshot from Yahoo! (www.yahoo.co.uk).

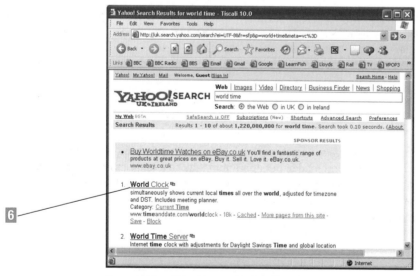

Screenshot from Yahoo! (www.yahoo.co.uk).

8.5.2 Running an Advanced Search

1 Load the site at http://uk.search.yahoo.com.

2 Click on the Advanced Search link.

3 Use the boxes and drop-down menus in the 'Show results with' section to list the keywords you want to find or ignore.

4 Click on the Updated drop-down menu to choose the time-frame in which the sites should have been updated.

5 Click on the button for the Site or Domain in which you want to search.

6 Click on the File Format drop-down menu to choose which format you want to search for.

7 Click on the appropriate button to choose whether to have your results filtered by SafeSearch.

8 Click on the drop-down menu to choose which Country to search through.

9 Click on the boxes next to the Language you want the found pages to be written in.

10 Click on the Number of Results drop-down menu to specify how many results you want found on each page.

11 Click on the Yahoo! Search button.

Screenshot from Yahoo! (www.yahoo.co.uk).

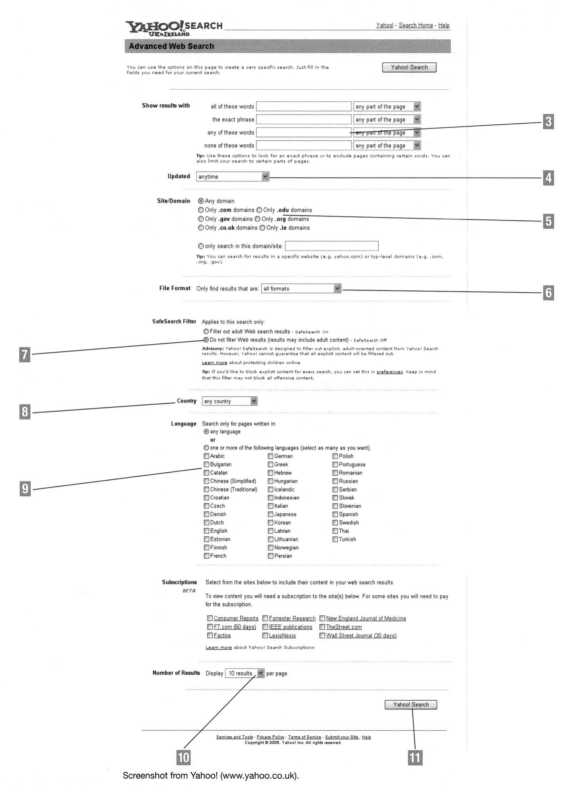

Screenshot from Yahoo! (www.yahoo.co.uk).

8.6 Using Google Local

You can use Google Local (http://local.google.co.uk) to find services in your local area. The site works in much the same way as the main Google site, except you have the extra option of specifying a location. So, you can use the site to find a plumber in Poole or a builder in Birmingham.

Once you've made a search, you'll not only get a list of results but also a map showing where all the businesses are located.

8.6.1 Using Google Local

1 Load the site in your browser (http://local.google.co.uk).

2 Type into the box what you're looking for and where (e.g. builder in Manchester).

3 Click on the 'Search' button.

4 Click on the buttons on the map to view details of that business.

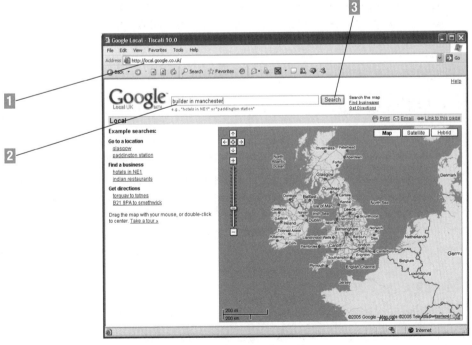

By kind permission of Google (www.google.co.uk).

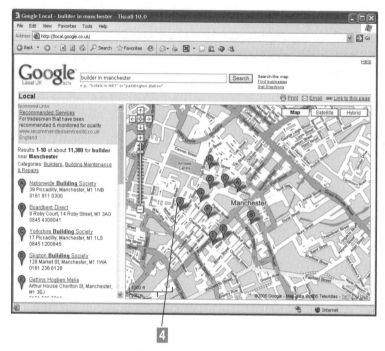

By kind permission of Google (www.google.co.uk).

Check the map

Once your results appear on Google Local, you are also presented with a map. Click on the arrow buttons on the map to move around it – or click on the 'Satellite' button to see a satellite photograph of the area you are viewing.

8.7 Using Singingfish

The best-known search engines are the likes of Yahoo! and Google, which search the whole of the web. However there are thousands more specialist search engines.

Singingfish is an excellent example of a specialist search engine – as it looks only for music and video files. Let's say you want to find some music files by your favourite band. You could use a mainstream searcher, but that will also find stacks of pages on that band, rather than actual songs.

Head onto Singingfish instead and you'll be able to limit your search to find only music files.

8.7.1 Finding Multimedia Files

1 Open the Singingfish site (www.singingfish.com) in your browser.

2 Click on the Search For drop-down menu and choose what you want to search for (just audio, just video or both).

3 Type into the search box some keywords that describe what you want to find.

4 Click on the Fish it button.

5 Click on the link of the file you want to watch/listen to.

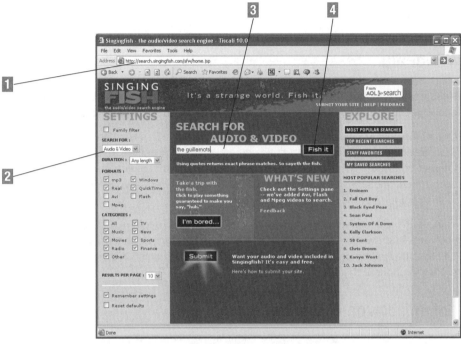

By kind permission of Singingfish (www.singingfish.com).

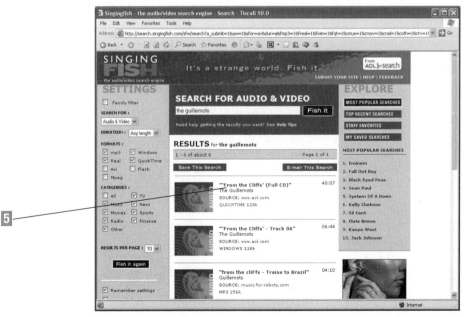

By kind permission of Singingfish (www.singingfish.com).

You will need to have the correct software to play multimedia files

If you want to play video and audio files on your computer, you'll need to have some player software on your computer. If you don't have the correct software, you'll see a warning message directing you to a site where you can download the program you need.

8.8 | Using Wikipedia

Need to settle a bet or help the kids with their homework? There are stacks of online encylopedias around that can help – and most can be accessed for free.

One of the best known and fastest growing is Wikipedia. This is an online reference guide that has been created by a team of volunteers, and which can be edited by anyone with an Internet connection. The result is a site with literally millions of entries covering a huge spectrum of subjects. It's like having your own encyclopedia in your house without having to shell out for a brand new bookcase.

You use the site in just the same way as a regular search engine – just type in the subject you want to know more about and click the search button. Once the results pop up, you'll be presented with a detailed description of your subject, which is cross-referenced to other entries throughout the site.

8.8.1　Finding Information on Wikipedia

1　Open the Wikipedia (www.wikipedia.com) site in your browser.

2　Type what you want to find out about in the Search box.

3　Click on the Go button.

4　Click on the subject you want if there is more than one match.

5　Scroll through the entry and click on any links that interest you.

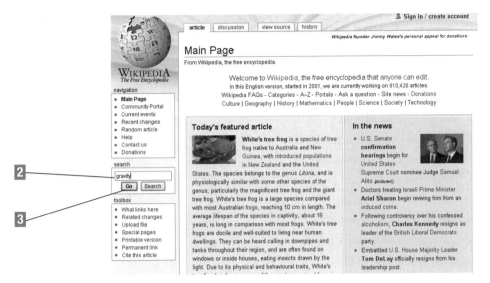

Screenshot from Wikipedia (www.wikipedia.org).

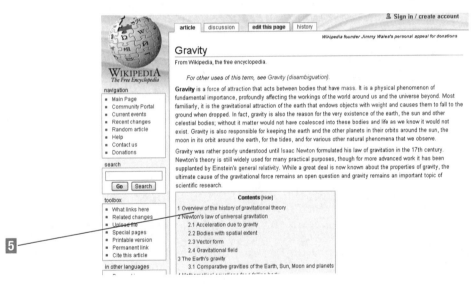

Screenshot from Wikipedia (www.wikipedia.org).

8.9 Handy Search Engine Links

Search engines

Google – www.google.co.uk

Yahoo! – http://uk.yahoo.com

Ask Jeeves – http://uk.ask.com/

AlltheWeb.com – www.alltheweb.com

HotBot – www.hotbot.co.uk

Teoma – www.teoma.co.uk

Altavista – www.altavista.co.uk

LookSmart – www.looksmart.com

Lycos – www.lycos.co.uk

MSN Search – http://search.msn.co.uk

Excite UK – www.excite.co.uk

WebCrawler – www.webcrawler.com

Dogpile – www.dogpile.co.uk

MetaCrawler – www.metacrawler.com

AOL Search – http://search.aol.com

CHAPTER 9

News Sites

9.1 Introduction

Give your paperboy an extra big tip next Christmas – he might not be in a job for much longer. Now you're online you need never buy a newspaper again, as there are thousands of free news sites all over the web. These are updated constantly, so you can always be bang up to date with what's happening in the world.

One of the biggest is the BBC's own news site – from where you can read all the latest headlines, and also access video and audio coverage of breaking stories.

All the major UK newspapers also have their own sites. These are constantly updated and include much of the content available in their print versions. Some of these news sites might require you to pay to access premium content, but these are few and far between.

The beauty of reading the news online is that you can then interact with it. For instance, if you read a story on the BBC site that you feel particularly strongly about, you can post a comment at the end of the report – which will then be available for everyone else to read.

9.2 Using the BBC Site

The BBC website isn't just about news. It is an enormous project filled with unbelievable amounts of content on all kinds of subjects. However, the news section of the site is one of the best to be found anywhere on the Internet.

You can quickly find news headlines from around the world on here, but you can also reduce your scope until the site is showing just the news headlines for the area in which you live.

The site is updated constantly throughout the day, so it's a great page to have bookmarked as one of your favourites.

9.2.1 Using BBC News

1 Load up the BBC site (www.bbc.co.uk) in your browser.

2 Click on the News link.

3 Click on the news category you want to read.

4 Click on the headline of the story you want to read.

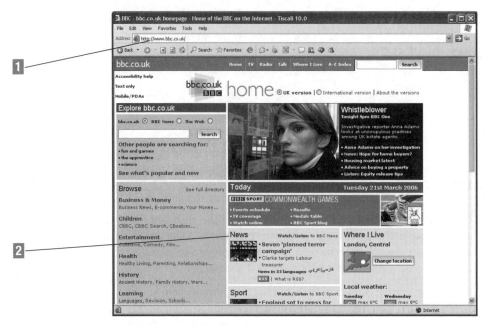

Screenshot from BBC (www.bbc.co.uk).

Screenshot from BBC (www.bbc.co.uk).

9.2.2 Finding Local News Sites Via BBC News

1 Load up the BBC site (www.bbc.co.uk) in your browser.

2 Click on the News link.

3 Click on the UK country you live in on the left.

4 Click on the News Where you Live drop-down menu on the right of the page (note: this only works for England and Wales at the moment).

5 Click on your area.

6 Click on the More news sites link.

7 Click on the site you wish to view.

Screenshot from BBC (www.bbc.co.uk).

Screenshot from BBC (www.bbc.co.uk).

Screenshot from BBC (www.bbc.co.uk).

Screenshot from BBC (www.bbc.co.uk).

Using Reuters

Reuters is a huge company that supplies news around the world. Of course, it also has its own website. Though most news sites also include lots of additional content, Reuters sticks to news and nothing but.

Where it excels is in delivering stories you might not find anywhere else. Those with their noses often in the FT will find it's also particularly good for business news.

If you've got a spare few minutes during the day, you should also take a look at the Oddly Enough section which is full of slightly quirky stories.

9.3.1 Reading a Story on Reuters

1 Load the Reuters site (www.reuters.co.uk) in your browser.

2 Click on the category you want to view from the list on the left.

3 Click on the headline of the story you want to read.

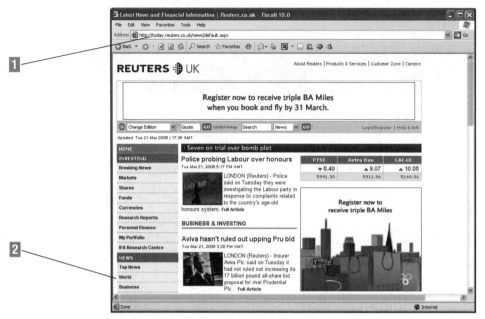

By kind permission of Reuters (www.reuters.co.uk).

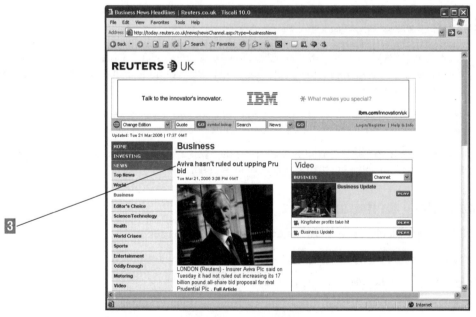

By kind permission of Reuters (www.reuters.co.uk).

A thousand words...

Be sure to click on the Pictures category on the Reuters website. This contains all the best Reuters photographs from every day of the past month – and there are some truly striking images to be seen.

Posting Comments to BBC Stories

One of the many extra features on the BBC News site is the option to add your own comments to certain news stories. The site's staff take a look at all submitted comments and, if they fit within guidelines, add them to the bottom of the published story. The comments are then available to be read by anyone who clicks onto the story.

9.4.1 Adding your Comments to a BBC Story

1 Load the BBC News site (www.bbc.co.uk/news) in your browser.

2 Click on the Have Your Say link on the left.

3 Click on the story you want to comment on.

4 Click on the Add Your Comment button.

5 Fill in the form with your details and your comment.

6 Click on the Add Your Comment button.

Screenshot from BBC (www.bbc.co.uk).

3

Screenshot from BBC (www.bbc.co.uk).

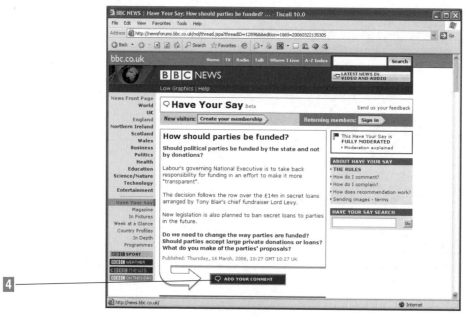

4

Screenshot from BBC (www.bbc.co.uk).

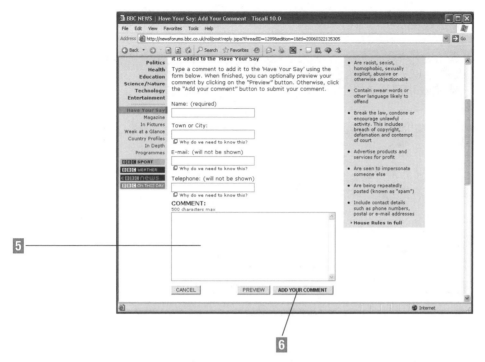

Screenshot from BBC (www.bbc.co.uk).

9.5 Voting on Interactive Polls

Another way of interacting with the news online is to vote on a web-based opinion poll. You'll find polls on most news sites, posing a question about an issue that's currently making headlines.

It's easy to have your say – you just need to click on the response you most agree with. Once you've done that, you go to a page which shows you the current results. New polls are regularly added to the BBC's Have Your Say pages.

9.5.1 Voting on Have Your Say

1 Load the BBC News site (www.bbc.co.uk/news) in your browser.

2 Click on the Have Your Say link on the left.

3 Click on the radio button next to the option you agree with on the poll.

4 Click on the Vote! button.

Screenshot from BBC (www.bbc.co.uk).

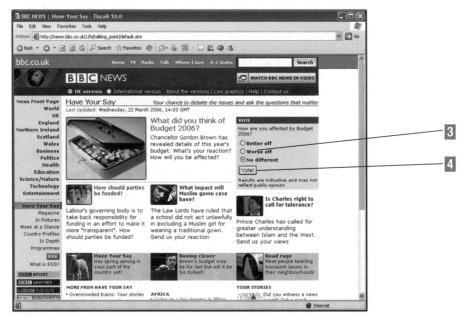

Screenshot from BBC (www.bbc.co.uk).

Sending In Feedback

Some sites might not have message boards or online polls set up. In this case you can often send your thoughts directly to the news provider, using a feedback form.

Local newspapers often have this kind of set-up, which gives you the option to contact the editor of the paper directly via the website. For an example, take a look at the site of Brighton newspaper *The Argus*.

9.6.1 Sending In Feedback

1 Load up *The Argus* website (www.theargus.co.uk).

2 Click on the Feedback link.

3 Click on the page link (in red font) to write a letter to the editor.

4 Fill in the form.

5 Click on the Send letter button.

By kind permission of *The Argus* (www.theargus.co.uk).

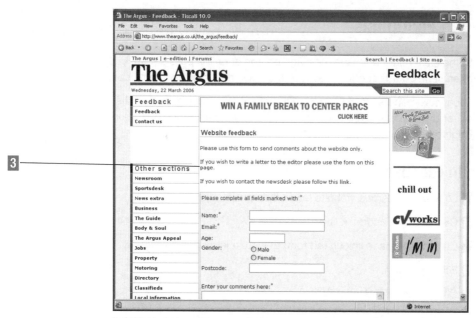

By kind permission of *The Argus* (www.theargus.co.uk).

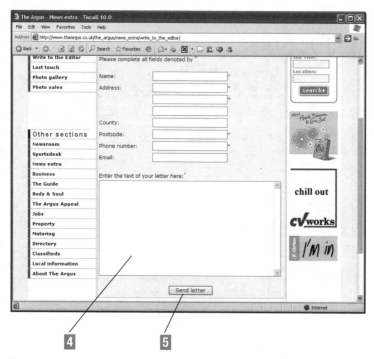

By kind permission of *The Argus* (www.theargus.co.uk).

9.7 Handy News Site Links

Online news sites

BBC News – www.bbc.co.uk/news

Reuters – www.reuters.co.uk

Google News – http://google.news.co.uk

NewsNow – www.newsnow.co.uk

Ananova – www.ananova.com

Online newspapers

The Telegraph – www.telegraph.co.uk

Guardian Unlimited – www.guardian.co.uk

The Independent – www.independent.co.uk

The Sun – www.thesun.co.uk

Daily Mirror – www.mirror.co.uk

Daily Mail – www.dailymail.co.uk

Foreign news sites

CNN.com – www.cnn.com

FOXNews.com – www.foxnews.com

9

CHAPTER 10

Government Sites

10.1 Introduction

As far as exciting pursuits go, surfing the Net for information on the government sounds roughly as thrilling as painting your house with a toothbrush. But wait! Although the rapidly expanding numbers of government sites on the Net might not get your heart racing, they can certainly make your life a lot easier, and perhaps even save you some cash into the bargain.

The hub of the government sites is DirectGov. Load up this site and you can instantly access links to all the government pages on the web. You can also make use of a truckload of information and features, enabling you to do anything from digging up the email address of your local councillor to booking your driving test online. There are also pages devoted to giving you information on what benefits or tax breaks you are entitled to.

It's possible to download all sorts of forms, which can then be printed out and posted off. For instance, you can quickly find the paperwork you need to have yourself added to the electoral roll.

Registering for your own online account at the Government Gateway site opens up even more options. Once you've registered, one of the tasks you can deal with online is the completion of your tax return, saving yourself hours of paperwork and headscratching.

Businesses get their very own government site, called Business Link. This is aimed at helping the owners of small/medium-sized businesses to find out more on running their company, making sure they're paying the right taxes and so on.

Then there are the more specialised sites, such as the Prime Minister's online home at the Number 10 site, where you can take a virtual tour of the premises and read up on the PM's latest speeches.

10.2 Using Directgov

Directgov is the central UK government site, from where you can access a range of online government services. Using this site you can find information on benefits, taxes, schools and so on.

You can also use the interactive services on the site to, for instance, book your driving test, renew your passport or tax your car – all via the Internet. The site is designed to make it easy to find out information about any area of the government. It also makes available contact details, so you can easily get in touch with any government department.

10.2.1 Finding Help on a Given Topic

1 Load the Directgov website (www.directgov.gov.uk) in your browser.

2 Click on the category you want in the Straight to… section.

3 Click on the links to get to the section you require.

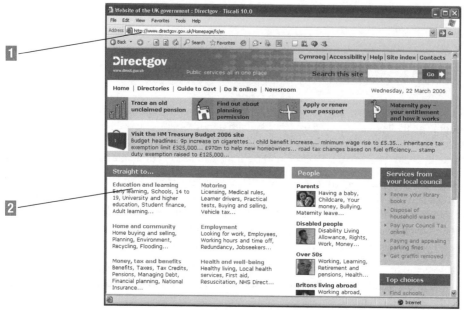

Crown copyright of Directgov (www.directgov.gov.uk).

Crown copyright of Directgov (www.directgov.gov.uk).

10.2.2 Finding Local Council Information

1 Load the Directgov website (www.directgov.gov.uk) in your browser.

2 Click on the Directories link at the top of the page.

3 Click on the Local Councils link.

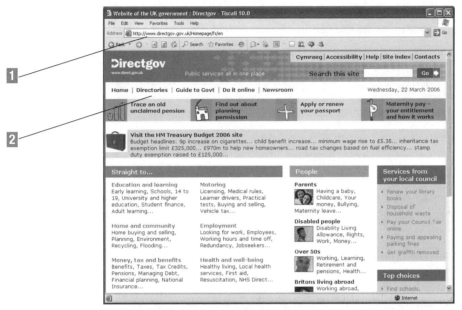

Crown copyright of Directgov (www.directgov.gov.uk).

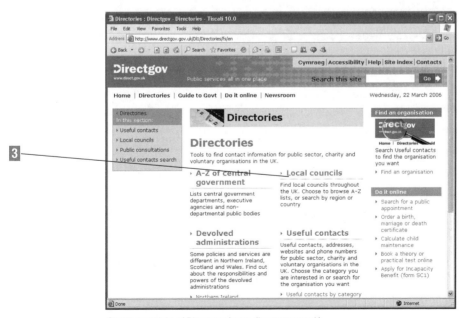

Crown copyright of Directgov (www.directgov.gov.uk).

4 Click on the area that covers the council you're after.

5 Click on the council name to access its details.

Crown copyright of Directgov (www.directgov.gov.uk).

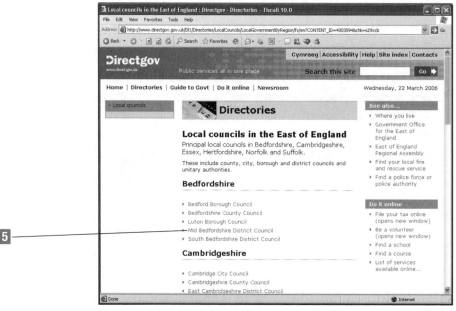

Crown copyright of Directgov (www.directgov.gov.uk).

10.2.3 Finding Government Department Information

1 Load the Directgov website (www.directgov.gov.uk) in your browser.

2 Click on the Directories link at the top of the page.

3 Click on the A-Z of Central Government link.

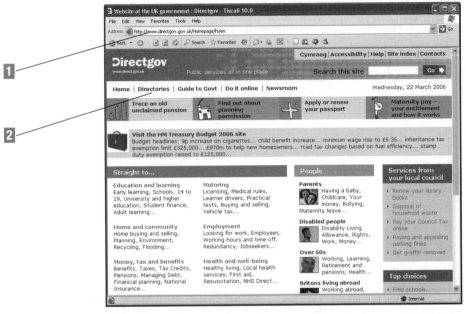

Crown copyright of Directgov (www.directgov.gov.uk).

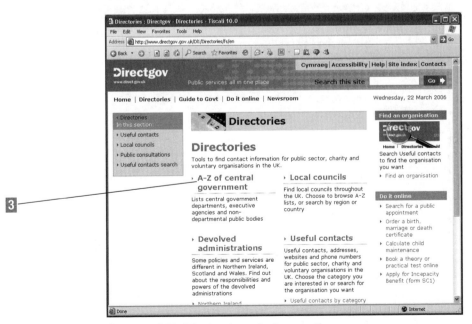

Crown copyright of Directgov (www.directgov.gov.uk).

4 Click on the initial letter of the department you're looking for.

5 Click on the department's name to access its details.

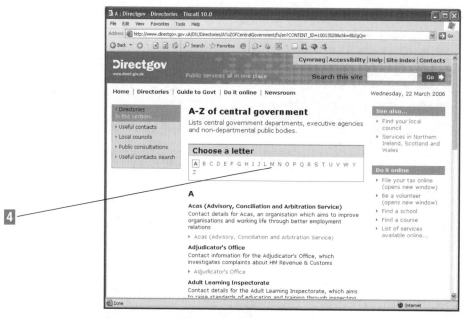

Crown copyright of Directgov (www.directgov.gov.uk).

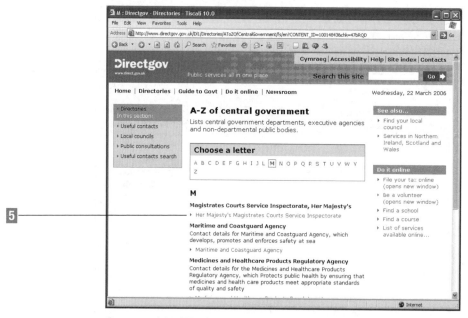

Crown copyright of Directgov (www.directgov.gov.uk).

10.2.4 Emailing a Government Department

1 Load the Directgov website (www.directgov.gov.uk) in your browser.

2 Click on the Contacts link.

3 Click on the Category that covers the department you want to email.

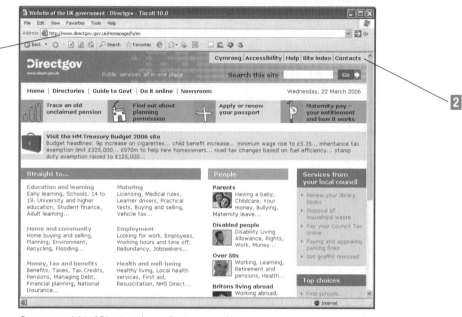

Crown copyright of Directgov (www.directgov.gov.uk).

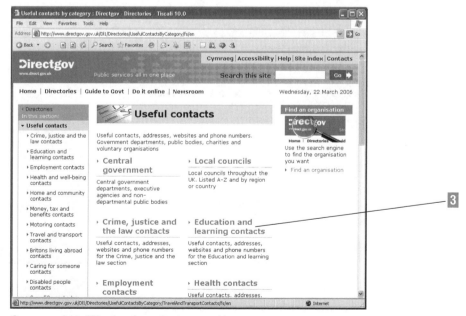

Crown copyright of Directgov (www.directgov.gov.uk).

4 Click on the department name you want to contact.

5 Click on the email address to open a new email addressed to that department.

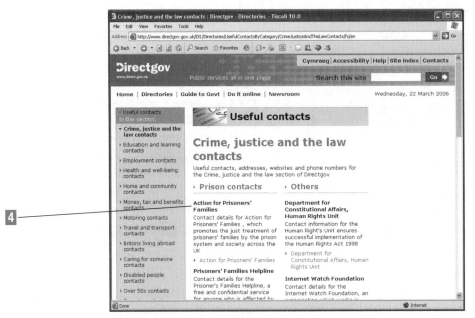

Crown copyright of Directgov (www.directgov.gov.uk).

Crown copyright of Directgov (www.directgov.gov.uk).

> **Not all departments will have email addresses**
>
> You may find there is no email address listed for the department you want to contact. However, you will always find phone and postal contact details.

10.3 | Using Business Link

Business Link is a government-run website designed to give advice to small and medium sized businesses. Whether you're running a successful company or just thinking about starting up, you can find advice on here on everything from paying your taxes to complying with health and safety regulations. The site also includes a handy search engine which will find the address of your local Business Link centre.

10.3.1 Navigating the Business Link Site

1 Load the Business Link site (www.businesslink.gov.uk) in your browser.

2 Click on the category name you want from the list.

3 Click on the link you want to find out more about the subject.

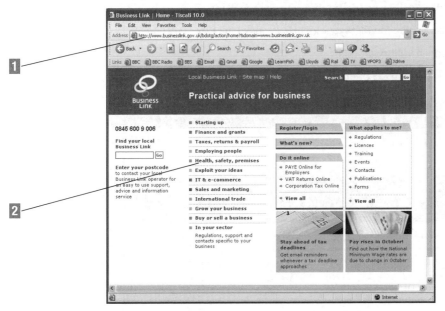

Crown copyright of Business Link (www.businesslink.gov.uk).

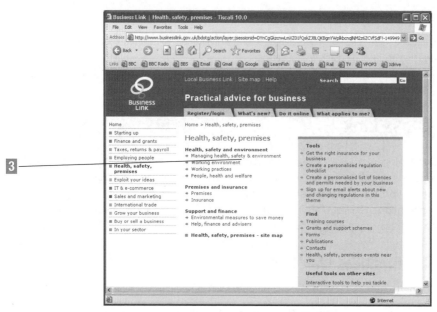

Crown copyright of Business Link (www.businesslink.gov.uk).

10.3.2 Finding your Local Business Link Branch

1 Click inside the Find your local Business Link box.

2 Type in your postcode.

3 Click on the Go button.

4 Click on the website link for the branch you want.

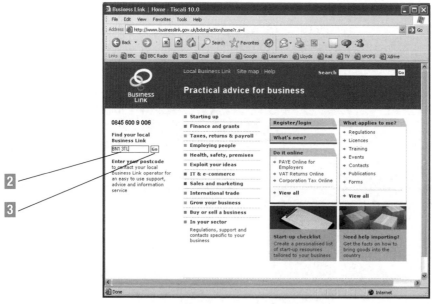

Crown copyright of Business Link (www.businesslink.gov.uk).

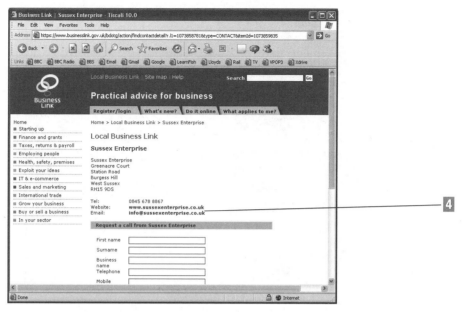

Crown copyright of Business Link (www.businesslink.gov.uk).

10.4 Visiting Number 10

The 10 Downing Street website gives you a window into the most famous address in the UK. This slick site is packed with information on all sorts of government issues, as well as detailed sections on the Prime Minister. You can access all the latest news from number ten, and even take a virtual tour around the inside of the building. Most of the information on the site can be accessed by clicking on the links at the top of the main page.

10.4.1 Sending an Email to the Prime Minister

1 Load the 10 Downing Street site (www.number-10.gov.uk) in your browser.

2 Click on the Contact link.

3 Click on the Via email option.

4 Click on the Choose Category drop-down menu.

5 Click on the subject you want to email about.

6 Click on the Go button.

7 Fill in the form.

8 Click on the Submit button.

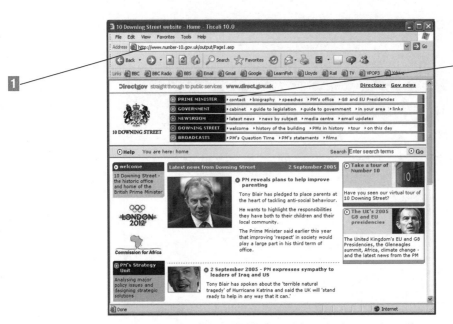

Crown copyright of the Office of Public Sector Information (www.opsi.gov.uk).

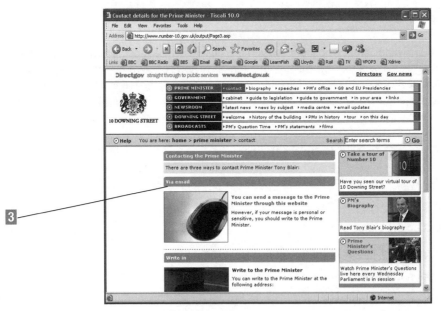

Crown copyright of the Office of Public Sector Information (www.opsi.gov.uk).

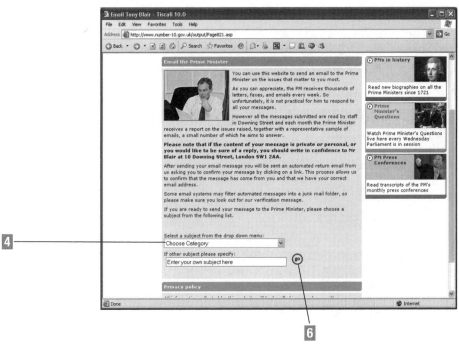

Crown copyright of the Office of Public Sector Information (www.opsi.gov.uk).

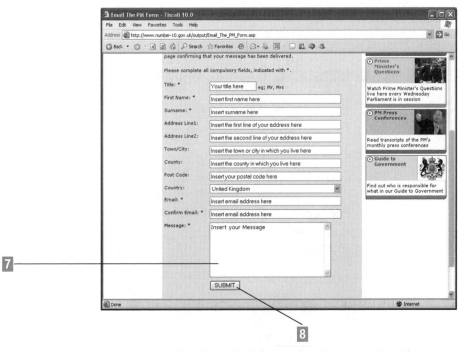

Crown copyright of the Office of Public Sector Information (www.opsi.gov.uk).

10.4.2 Finding Local Information

1 Load the 10 Downing Street site (www.number-10.gov.uk) in your browser.

2 Click on the 'in your area' link.

3 Click on your region.

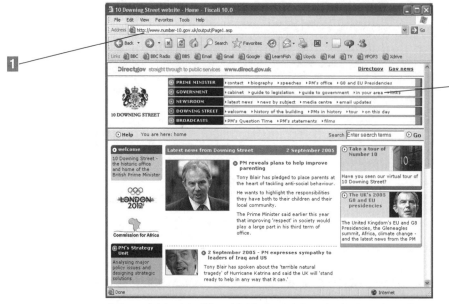

Crown copyright of the Office of Public Sector Information (www.opsi.gov.uk).

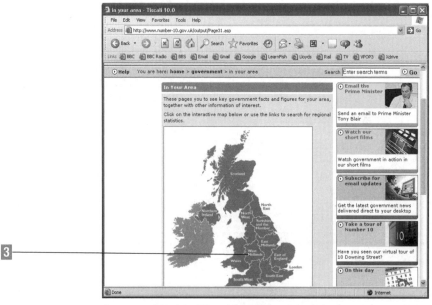

Crown copyright of the Office of Public Sector Information (www.opsi.gov.uk).

10.4.3 Take a Tour of Number 10

1 Load the 10 Downing Street site (www.number-10.gov.uk) in your browser.

2 Click on the 'tour' link.

3 Click on the links to go through the tour.

4 Click on any of the view links to take a proper look at that area.

5 When viewing an area, click and drag on the image to move around.

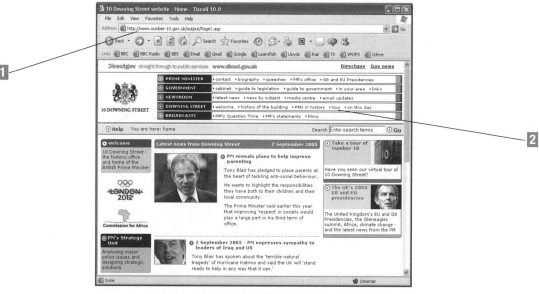

Crown copyright of the Office of Public Sector Information (www.opsi.gov.uk).

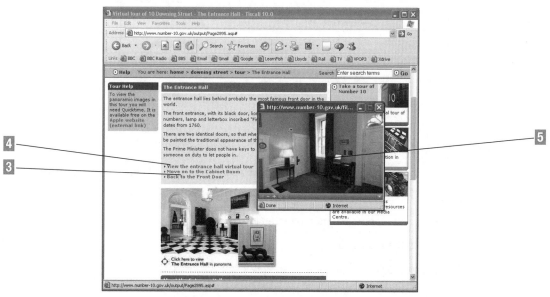

Crown copyright of the Office of Public Sector Information (www.opsi.gov.uk).

Visiting the Office of National Statistics

The mere mention of 'statistics' is enough to send non-maths boffins running for cover. But, like it or not, statistics rule our lives. This government site provides all the information you need on key subjects such as the latest inflation, employment and population figures.

The site has been designed to make it easy to find what you're after. For instance, you can search the site by theme. Hit the 'Economy' theme option and you'll find stats on everything from quality of life to share ownership.

10.5.1 Browsing the Key Statistics

1 Load the National Statistics Online (www.statistics.gov.uk) site in your browser.

2 Click on the link you require in the Key statistics section.

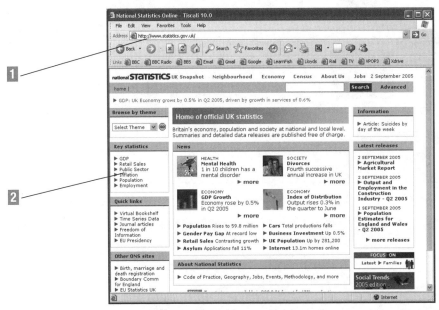

Source: National Statistics website (www.statistics.gov.uk).

10.5.2 Browsing Statistics by Theme

1 Load the National Statistics Online (www.statistics.gov.uk) site in your browser.

2 Click on the Select Theme drop-down menu.

3 Click on the theme you're interested in.

4 Click on the Go button.

5 Click on the link you want to read about.

Source: National Statistics website (www.statistics.gov.uk).

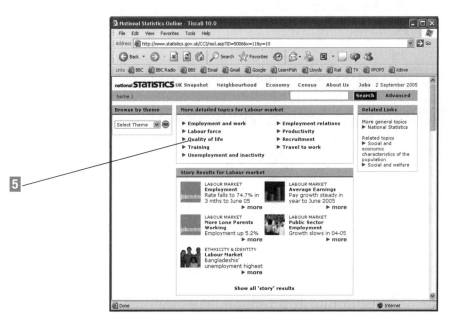

Source: National Statistics website (www.statistics.gov.uk).

10.6 | Registering to Vote

Voting booths will one day become a thing of the past, as we'll all be logging on to the Internet on election days to cast our votes electronically. However, that day is still some way off at the moment. Online voting will not happen until a completely foolproof system can be devised to prevent any possible cheating.

So, for now at least, we'll have to stick to the tried and tested method of ballot boxes and ticked pieces of paper. Where the Internet can already help is in updating your details on the Electoral Register. Although it's not possible to update those details entirely online, you can use the Net to download copies of all the forms you need.

10.6.1 Getting your Registration Forms

1 Load the About My Vote (www.aboutmyvote.co.uk) site in your browser.

2 Type your postcode into the box.

3 Click on the Enter Site button.

4 Click on the 'register to vote' link.

5 Click on the link that best describes you.

6 Click on the 'Download your registration form now' link.

7 Print out the form.

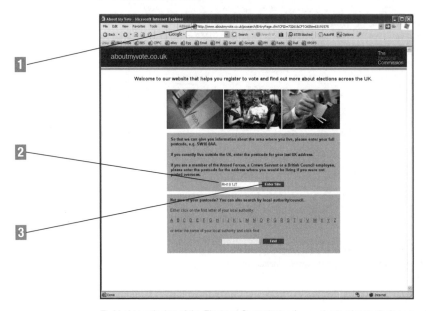

By kind permission of the Electoral Commission (www.electoralcommission.gov.uk).

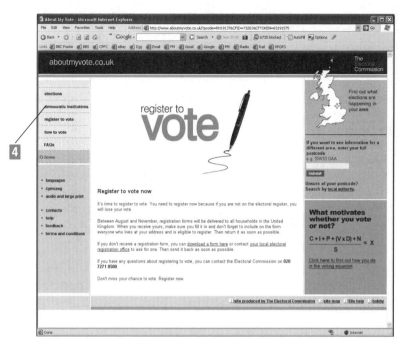

By kind permission of the Electoral Commission (www.electoralcommission.gov.uk).

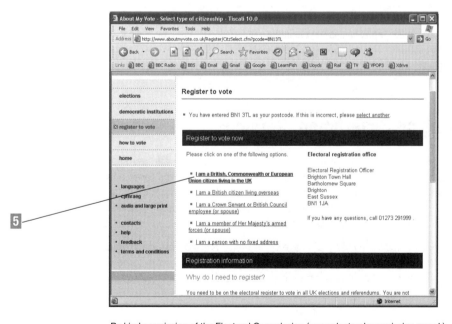

By kind permission of the Electoral Commission (www.electoralcommission.gov.uk).

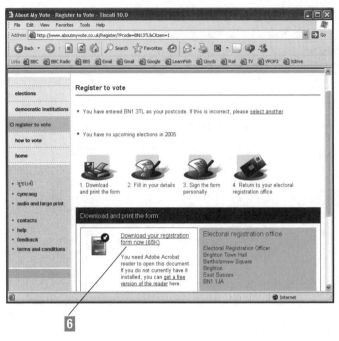

6

By kind permission of the Electoral Commission (www.electoralcommission.gov.uk).

Software you'll need

The registration forms on this site are in the .pdf format. This is a type of file that can only be read by certain software. The most popular pdf reader is produced by Adobe (www.adobe.com). Visit their site to download a free version of Adobe Reader.

10.7 Registering on Government Services

There are already several government services which you can access online – and the number is growing all the time. For instance, if you have to submit a tax return each year, you can do that via the Internet (so no need to sit there with a calculator and chewed pencil!). Or, you could use the Net to view your council tax bill, check up on your state pension, and so on. Over time, there will be far more services you will be able to use online.

But before you can use any of these online features, you need to register with the central Government Gateway site. By doing this, you'll be issued with some unique log-in details, which you can use to access the various services.

10.7.1 Registering on Government Sites

1 Load the Government Gateway site (www.gateway.gov.uk) in your browser.

2 Click on the 'Register as an Individual' link.

3 Click on the 'Register with a User ID' button.

4 Fill in all the fields on the form, then click on the Continue button.

5 Click on the boxes next to the services you want to sign up for, then click Continue.

6 Fill in the form that appears (this will vary depending on the options you chose in the previous steps).

7 Click Continue again.

8 Click on the Continue button once more, then make a note of your User ID.

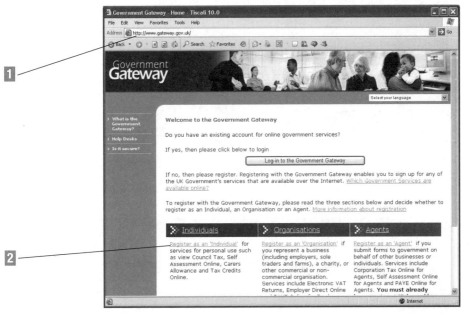

Crown copyright material is reproduced with the permission of the controller of HMSO.

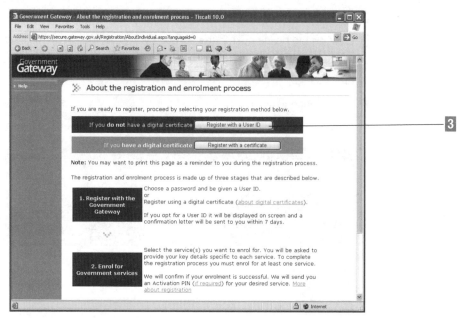

Crown copyright material is reproduced with the permission of the controller of HMSO.

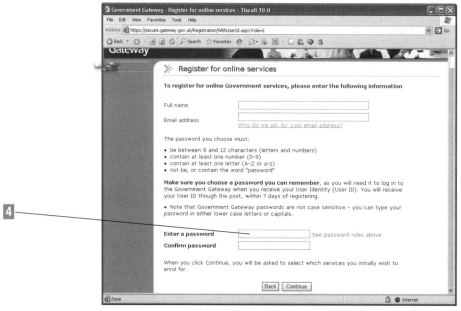

Crown copyright material is reproduced with the permission of the controller of HMSO.

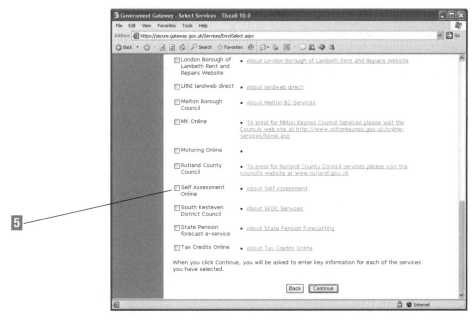

Crown copyright material is reproduced with the permission of the controller of HMSO.

Watch your doormat!

Your registration isn't complete until you receive your Activation PIN number – which will be sent to you through the post. Once your number arrives, you need to return to the Government Gateway site to activate your account.

10.8 Handy Government Site Links

UK Government sites

Directgov – www.directgov.gov.uk

Business Link – www.businesslink.gov.uk

10 Downing Street – www.number-10.gov.uk

National Statistics Online – www.statistics.gov.uk

About My Vote – www.aboutmyvote.co.uk

Government Gateway site – www.gateway.gov.uk

Local Government Association – www.lga.gov.uk

Devolved governments

National Assembly for Wales – www.wales.gov.uk

Scottish Executive – www.scotland.gov.uk

Northern Ireland Office – www.nio.gov.uk

CHAPTER 11

Shopping and Leisure

11.1 Introduction

There aren't many people out there who actually enjoy going to the local supermarket for the weekly shop. Most, in fact, find the whole process to be fraught with hair-tearing frustrations. If you manage to avoid picking the wobbly-wheeled trolley, you've still got to put up with the heaving crowds and screaming toddlers that populate the aisles of your nearest food emporium.

So what a relief that here is yet another task from which the Internet can rescue you. These days most major food-stores have their own websites. By logging on, you can do your shop from the comfort of your own home and then have it delivered straight to your door. The whole process is very simple and just involves clicking on the items you want to buy.

Of course, it's not just food shopping which you can do online. There are thousands more Internet stores selling everything under the sun. One of the most popular and well-known is Amazon – a huge site from where you can buy CDs, games, books and more. Again, whatever bargains you dig up are delivered direct to your home. You need never go near the high street again.

To get all that shopping done, you're going to need to keep an eye on your cashflow. That's easy too, as you can also use the Internet to do your banking. All the major banks now have their own online facilities, and you don't need to open a new account to use them. Simply head to your bank's website and enable your existing account for Internet transactions.

Once that's done, you can complete all kinds of money-related tasks via your bank's web-based branch. For instance, you can check your statements with just a couple of mouse clicks, pay off the gas bill, or set up a new direct debit. All the sorts of things that used to require you standing in line in your local branch for ages can now be done with a couple of mouse clicks.

The Internet is also a great way to find out what's going on in your local area. There are sites that will give you listings of all the events taking place round your way, from craft fairs to the latest blockbusters at the local mutliplex.

11.2 Using Online Banking

Until you've paid off your latest credit card bill in your pyjamas, you really haven't lived. All the major banks are now online, so it's easy to activate your bank account so you can access it via the Internet. Get in touch with your local branch or simply visit the website of your bank to set up your online account. Once you're up and running, you can get up to all kinds of bank-related antics at any time of the day or night – with no need to queue!

You don't have to sign up to see how online banking works – most sites will include a demo feature which gives you a feel for how the service works. Here, we'll show you how to use the features on the LloydsTSB website. You'll find that all the other online banking sites work in a similar way.

11.2.1 Using Online Banking Demos

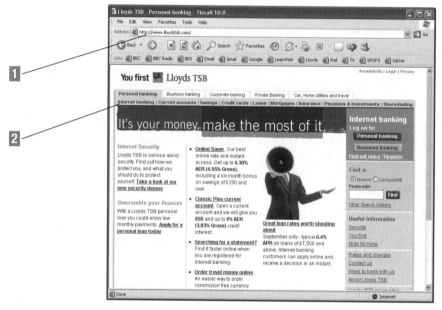

Screenshot from LloydsTSB (www.lloydstsb.com).

1 Load the LloydsTSB site (www.lloydstsb.co.uk) in your browser.

2 Click on the Internet banking link.

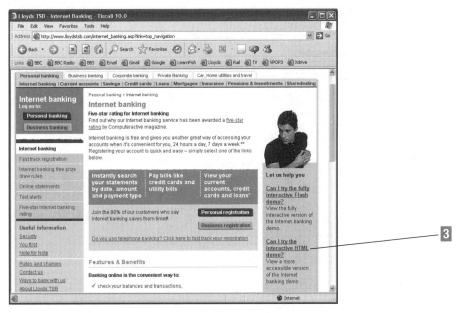

Screenshot from LloydsTSB (www.lloydstsb.com).

3 Click on the 'Can I try the interactive HTML demo?' link.

4 The demo feature will open in a separate window. On the left is a help section that explains what each part of the banking feature does.

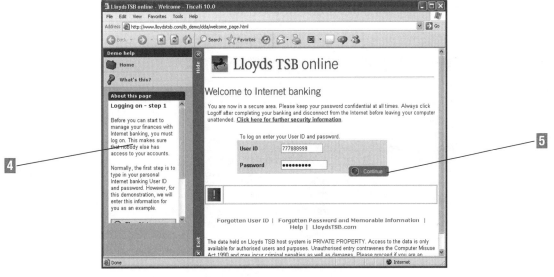

Screenshot from LloydsTSB (www.lloydstsb.com).

5 Click on the Continue button twice to get through to the main banking screen.

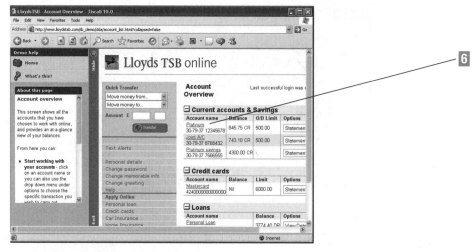

Screenshot from LloydsTSB (www.lloydstsb.com).

6 Click on the name of the account you want to view.

11.2.2 Registering for Online Banking

1 Load the LloydsTSB site (www.lloydstsb.co.uk) in your browser.

2 Click on the Register link.

3 Click on Personal registration.

4 Fill in the form and click on the Send button.

5 The bank will get in touch with you to complete your registration.

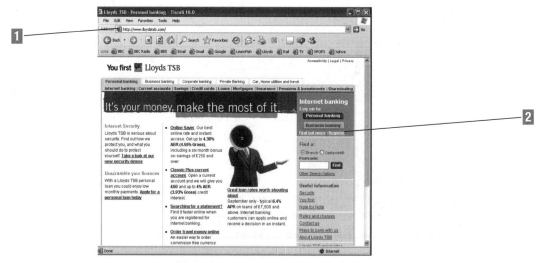

Screenshot from LloydsTSB (www.lloydstsb.com).

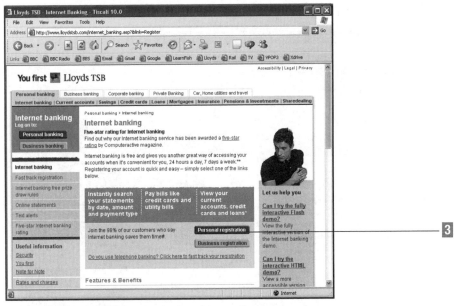

Screenshot from LloydsTSB (www.lloydstsb.com).

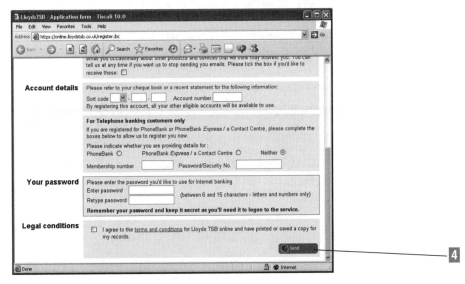

Screenshot from LloydsTSB (www.lloydstsb.com).

Take careful note of the password you choose

During the registration process, you'll be asked to come up with a password. Make it something difficult to guess – combinations of letters and numbers are good, for example, jer54teq23. But make sure it's something you can remember easily, as you'll need this information to log onto the site once you're registered.

11.2.3 Logging in for Real

Screenshot from LloydsTSB (www.lloydstsb.com).

1 Load the LloydsTSB site (www.lloydstsb.co.uk) in your browser.

2 Click on the Log on to: Personal banking button.

3 Fill in your User ID and password, then click Continue.

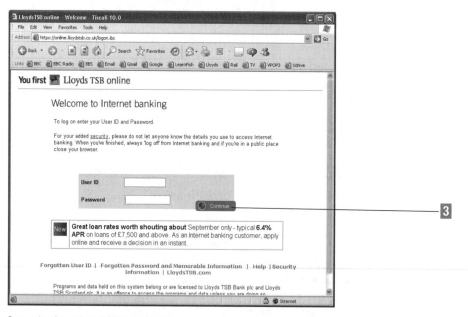

Screenshot from LloydsTSB (www.lloydstsb.com).

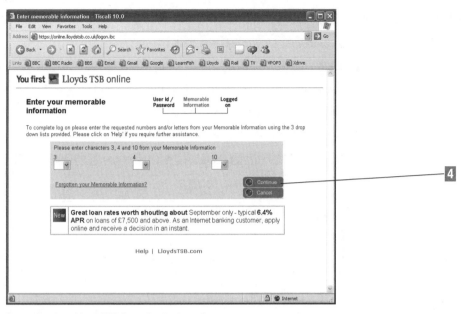

Screenshot from LloydsTSB (www.lloydstsb.com).

4 Fill in the requested letters from your Memorable Information, then click Continue.

5 Click on the name of the account you want to view.

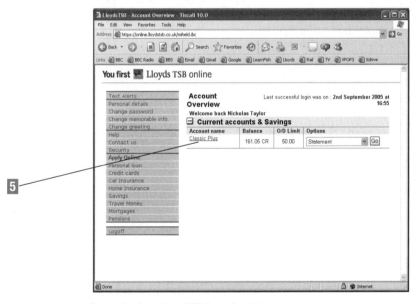

Screenshot from LloydsTSB (www.lloydstsb.com).

11.2.4 Transferring Money Between your Accounts

1 Log onto your LloydsTSB account.

2 Click on the Move money from... drop-down list and click on the relevant account.

3 Click on the Move money to... drop-down list and click on the relevant account.

4 Type in the amount you want to transfer.

5 Click on the Transfer button.

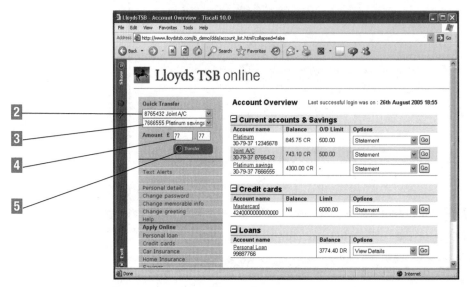

Screenshot from LloydsTSB (www.lloydstsb.com).

11.2.5 Pay a Bill Online

1 Log onto your LloydsTSB account.

2 Click on the account you want to pay the bill from.

3 Click on the Transfers & Payments link.

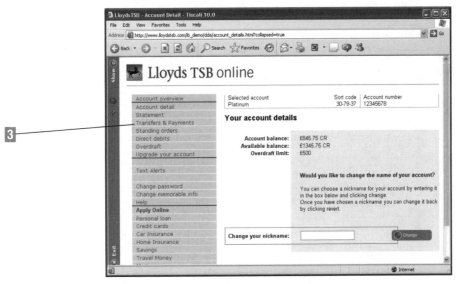

Screenshot from LloydsTSB (www.lloydstsb.com).

4 Click on the link that reads Click here to add a new recipient to the list.

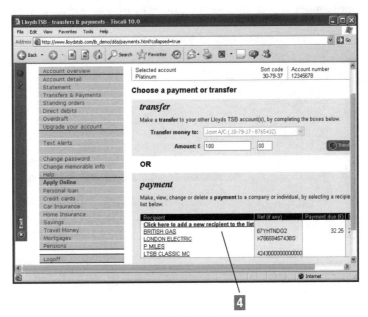

Screenshot from LloydsTSB (www.lloydstsb.com).

5 Click on the Pay a Bill option.

6 Type the name into the company box then click on the Find company button.

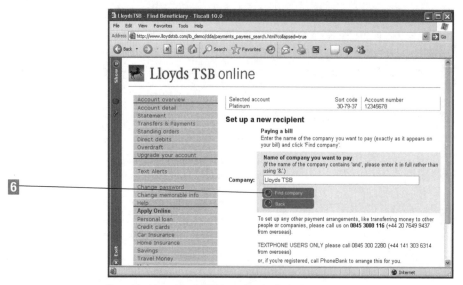

Screenshot from LloydsTSB (www.lloydstsb.com).

7 Click on the correct company from the list.

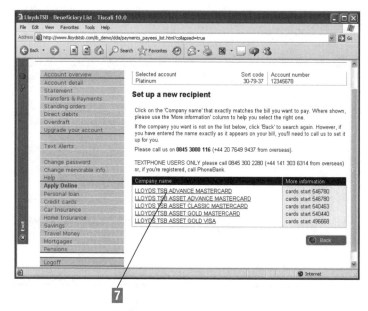

Screenshot from LloydsTSB (www.lloydstsb.com).

8 Type in the correct reference number (normally your account number with the company you're paying).

9 Click on the Add to my list button.

10 Click on the Here link.

11 Type in the correct payment details, then click on the Change payment button.

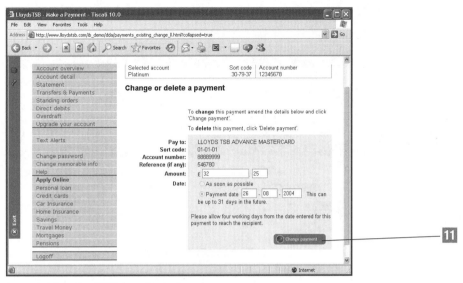

Screenshot from LloydsTSB (www.lloydstsb.com).

12 Type in your password, then click on the Confirm button.

Paying the same company again

Once you've gone through the above process, the company you've paid will be added to your own personal list. Next time you go to make a payment, you'll be able to simply click on the company's name, rather than running a search for it.

11.3 Shopping on Amazon

Wave bye-bye to those crowded high streets, never-ending queues and surly shop assistants. Now you're online you can do all your shopping from the comfort of your own home. There are stores on the Net selling everything you could ever need. You can do all your grocery shopping by visiting the sites of the big-name supermarkets (who will deliver all those heavy bags direct to your doorstep). You can snap up all the clothes you want from any of the high-street names, and go shoe-shopping without wearing out any shoe leather. You'll find stores devoted to selling nothing but cheese, tiny shops that specialise in chilli sauce, and sites from which you can only buy kites.

In short, there's a store out there that can cater for anything you want to buy. Best of all, you'll find the prices of these shops are often a chunk cheaper than what you'd find in a regular shop. King of the online stores is Amazon. This gargantuan site started life selling books, but now knocks out anything from CDs to vacuum cleaners.

11.3.1 Buying From Amazon

1 Load up the Amazon UK (www.amazon.co.uk) site in your browser.

2 Click on the category in which you want to shop.

Screenshot from Amazon (www.amazon.co.uk).

3 Click through the sub-categories to find what you want.

4 Click on the item you want to buy.

Screenshot from Amazon (www.amazon.co.uk).

5 Click on the Add to Shopping Basket link.

6 Click on the Proceed to Checkout button.

Screenshot from Amazon (www.amazon.co.uk).

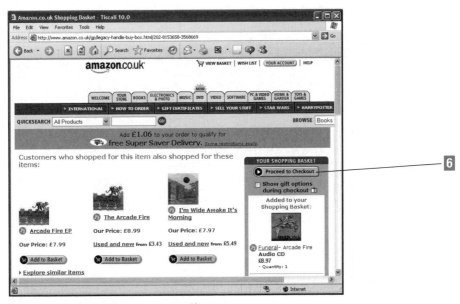

Screenshot from Amazon (www.amazon.co.uk).

7 Type your email address into the box, then click on the I am a new customer button.

8 Click on the Sign in... button.

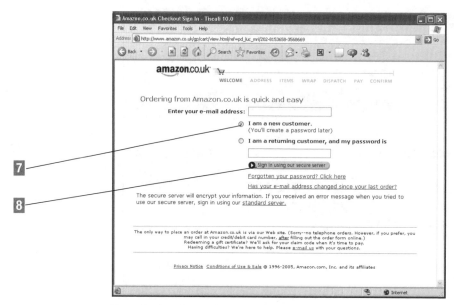

Screenshot from Amazon (www.amazon.co.uk).

9 Fill in the form, then click Continue.

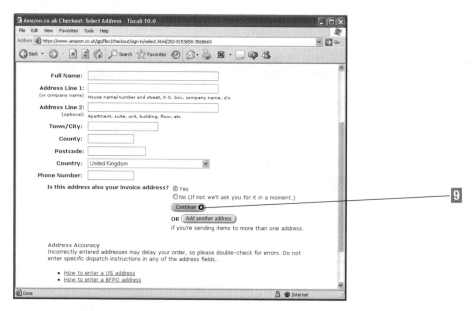

Screenshot from Amazon (www.amazon.co.uk).

10 Fill in the next form, including your credit card details, then click on the Continue button.

11 Click on the Place your order button.

11.3.2 Searching Through Amazon Quickly

1 Load up the Amazon UK site (www.amazon.co.uk) in your browser.

2 Click inside the search box and type the name of what you're after.

3 Click on the All Products drop-down menu and select the category your item falls into.

4 Click on the Go! Button.

5 Click on the link for the item you're after.

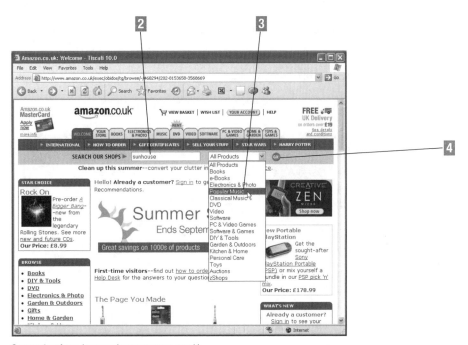

Screenshot from Amazon (www.amazon.co.uk).

Bag yourself free delivery

Some sites will always offer free delivery of your shopping but others, such as Amazon, will charge. The charge is dependent on how many items you buy, how heavy they are and so on. However, you'll often find you qualify for free delivery if you spend over a certain amount on the site. On Amazon, you currently need to shell out more than £15 to qualify. Bear in mind items sent by free delivery will often take longer to arrive.

11.4 Finding Local Events

Next time you find yourself at home twiddling your thumbs, hop on the Net to find something to do in your local area. There are stacks of sites on the Internet which list local events going on in your region, the latest cinema times, what's on at the theatre, and so on.

A visit to the excellent Whatsonwhen website can trawl up events from anywhere in the world. For instance, if you're going on holiday you can run a search for any events happening in the area you're visiting within the dates you will be there.

11.4.1 Finding Local Events on Whatsonwhen

1 Load the Whatsonwhen site (www.whatsonwhen.com) in your browser.

2 Scroll down the page to the Search box.

3 Fill in the fields of the form to show what you want to search for.

4 Click on the Search button.

5 Click on any of the search results to find out more.

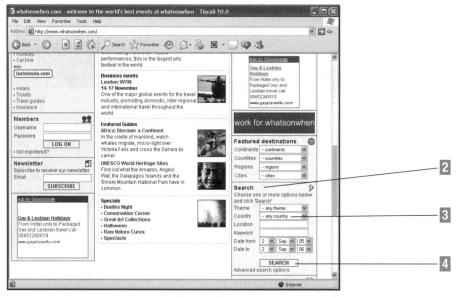

Screenshot reproduced with permission of Whatsonwhen Limited (www.whatsonwhen.com).

11.5 Handy Shopping and Leisure Site Links

Banks and building societies

LloydsTSB – www.lloydstsb.com

HSBC – www.hsbc.co.uk

Barclays – www.barclays.co.uk

Natwest – www.natwest.com

Abbey – www.abbey.com

Halifax – www.halifax.co.uk

Nationwide – www.nationwide.co.uk

Major shops

Play.com – www.play.com (CDs, DVDs, games)

bol.com – www.bol.com/uk (books)

Kelkoo – www.kelkoo.co.uk (price comparison)

Amazon – www.amazon.co.uk (books, CDs, electronics, etc)

eBay – www.ebay.co.uk (online auctions)

Going out

Virgin.net Movies – www.virgin.net/movies (local cinema listings)

Whatsonstage – www.whatsonstage.com (buy theatre tickets)

beerintheevening.com – www.beerintheevening.com (local pub reviews)

11

CHAPTER 12

Booking Travel

12.1 Introduction

Just as the advent of online shopping means you can opt out of Saturday trips to the town centre, so the availability of online travel stores mean you can give your travel agent the heave-ho.

Settle down in front of your PC monitor and you can quickly find cheap flights to anywhere in the world. You'll also be able to dig up low-priced hotel rooms or package deals which significantly undercut what you'll find elsewhere.

Consider companies such as easyJet and Ryanair, for example. These no-frills airlines have built their success around the growth of the Internet. Their cheap prices can be kept even cheaper because they take so many of their bookings via their websites. This means there is less need for expensive telesales centres and therefore fewer overheads. It's a model that's followed by many travel companies, and it means the savvy online traveller can save a stack of cash by shopping around the Net.

The beauty of all this is that shopping around is so easy. Once you've found a good deal, you can instantly click over to another site and find out whether they can beat it. You'll often find that by buying your flight tickets and hotel room separately, you'll be able to create a really impressive deal.

And it's not just your bank balance that can be helped out by researching your travel plans on the Internet. It's also easy to check travel timetables, whether for a transatlantic flight or tomorrow morning's commuter train.

12

12.2 Checking Train Times

There are several sites on the Internet that enable you to check through the timetables for all the train services in the country. Using these sites, you simply type in where you are travelling to and from. Next, you specify the time and date on which you want to travel, and the site will display a list of times that match the journey you need to make. Included with the results will be details of any train changes you need to make throughout your journey, as well as the total time it will take.

One of the most popular sites offering this service is National Rail Enquiries. Check your times on here and, once you've dug up the times you're after, you can then purchase the tickets online if you wish.

12.2.1 Checking National Rail Enquiries

1 Load the National Rail Enquiries site (www.nationalrail.co.uk) in your browser.

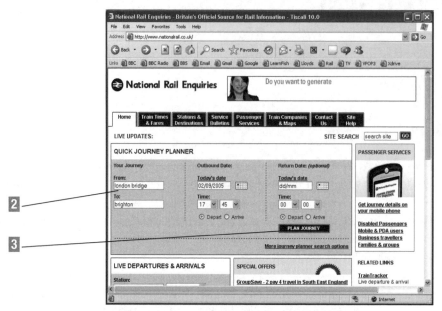

Screenshot from National Rail Enquiries (www.nationalrail.co.uk).

2 Fill in the form with the details of the journey you want to make.

3 Click on the Plan Journey button.

4 Click on the View Details button to check any train changes you need to make.

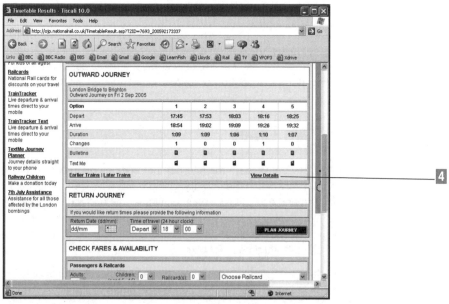

Screenshot from National Rail Enquiries (www.nationalrail.co.uk).

Further options

If you're making a very specific journey, click on the More journey planner search options link to bring up an advanced search page. Using this, you can specify the number of changes you're willing to make, as well as detailing any stations you wish to travel through, or avoid.

12.3 Booking Flights

Booking travel on the Internet is not only easy – it can also save you money. Get organised and book your flights a few months in advance and you could literally save hundreds of pounds. You can then book your hotel separately and end up paying far less than you would have done by buying a package.

There's a wide choice of sites out there selling flights. Some of them, such as ebookers, will search through a wide range of available flights for you and then display the best prices. Other sites, such as easyJet's, give results only for their own particular airline.

12.3.1 Booking a Flight on ebookers

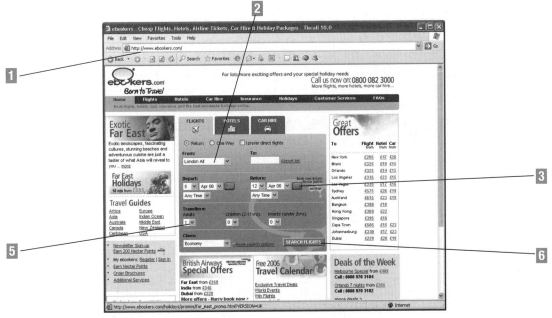

Screenshot from ebookers.com (www.ebookers.com).

1 Load the ebookers site (www.ebookers.com) in your browser.

2 Fill in the From and To fields on the form.

3 Click on the calendar icons to select the dates on which you want to leave and return.

4 Click on the arrow buttons to move through the months on the calendar, then click on the date you want.

5 Use the drop-down menus to complete the rest of the form.

6 Click on the Search Flights button.

7 Click on the Select button for the flight you want.

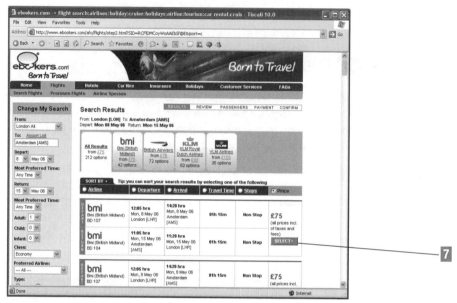

Screenshot from ebookers.com (www.ebookers.com).

8 Select the options you want from the following screen by clicking on the boxes.

9 Click on the Continue Booking button.

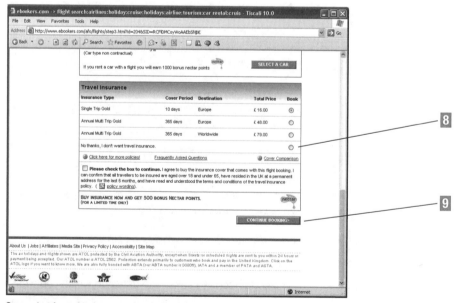

Screenshot from ebookers.com (www.ebookers.com).

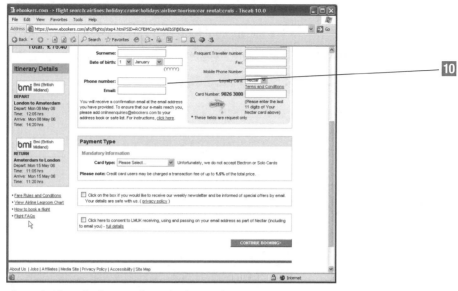

Screenshot from ebookers.com (www.ebookers.com).

10 Fill in the personal details forms on the next page, then click on the Continue Booking button.

11 Fill in your card details, then click on the Confirm Booking button.

12.3.2 Booking a Flight on easyJet

1 Load the easyJet site (www.easyjet.co.uk) in your browser.

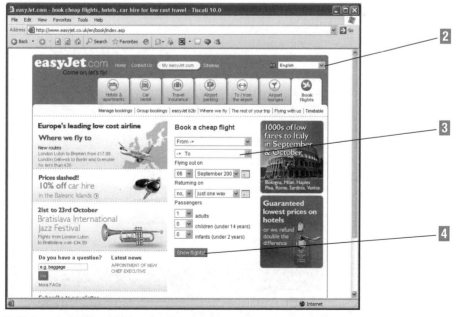

By kind permission of easyJet (www.easyjet.com).

2 Click on the language in which you wish to view the site.

3 Fill in the Book a cheap flight form with the details of the trip you want to make.

4 Click on the Show flights! button.

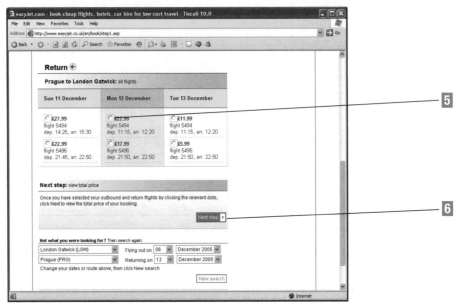

By kind permission of easyJet (www.easyjet.com).

5 Click on the circles next to the flights you want to take.

6 Click on the Next step button.

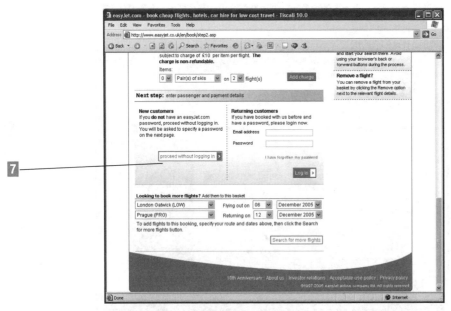

By kind permission of easyJet (www.easyjet.com).

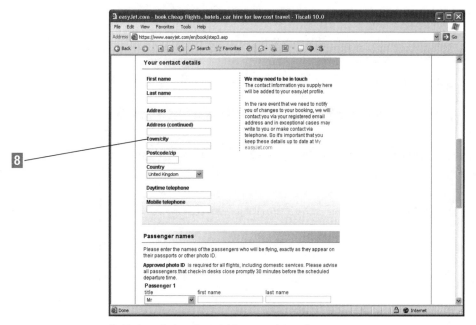

By kind permission of easyJet (www.easyjet.com).

7 Click on the Proceed without logging in button.

8 Fill in the form that appears, then click on the Book now button.

Booking early makes sense

When you're booking your own flight online, it makes sense to be quick. By booking early, you can take advantage of some really cheap prices. Most sites will increase the price of a flight as it becomes more full up, so it will cost you more – not less – if you wait until the last minute.

12.4 Booking Hotels

Whenever you need to stay in a hotel, it's a good idea to do some online research first. There are stacks of websites around which you can use to book a hotel room, so a quick spot of shopping around can soon find you some real bargains.

The great thing about booking your hotel in this way is that you've got complete flexibility over what you want. Just type in the place where you want to stay, then type in the dates you want to spend in the hotel. When you run the search, you'll get a list of all the hotels that have spare rooms that fit in with what you've asked for. With a click of the mouse, you can then sort these hotels so the cheapest is at the top – making it easy to search through them all by price.

12.4.1 Booking a Hotel on Expedia

Anyone can search for available hotels on Expedia, but to book anything you will first have to register with the site.

1 Load the Expedia site (www.expedia.co.uk) in your browser.

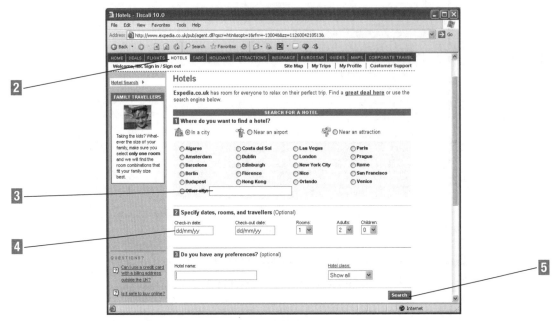

Screenshot from Expedia.co.uk (www.expedia.co.uk).

2 Click on the Hotels tab.

3 Type the name of the place in which you want to stay in the Other city box.

4 Fill in the rest of the form with the dates and number of people you are booking for.

5 Click on the Search button.

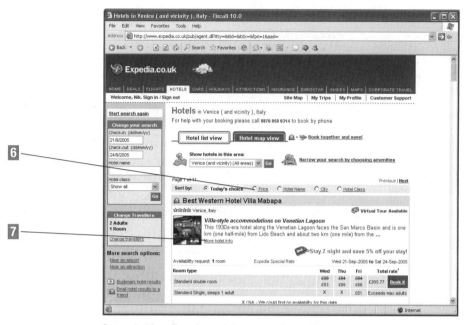

Screenshot from Expedia.co.uk (www.expedia.co.uk).

6 Click on the heading by which you would like to sort the hotels.

7 Click on the More hotel info button to find out more.

Screenshot from Expedia.co.uk (www.expedia.co.uk).

8 Click on the Continue to Booking button.

Screenshot from Expedia.co.uk (www.expedia.co.uk).

9 Click on the Book it button next to the room you would like.

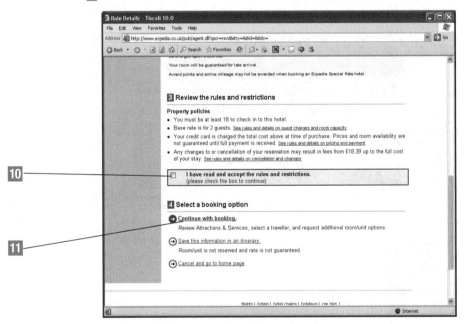

Screenshot from Expedia.co.uk (www.expedia.co.uk).

10 Click on the box to confirm you have read the terms and conditions.

11 Click on the Continue with booking button.

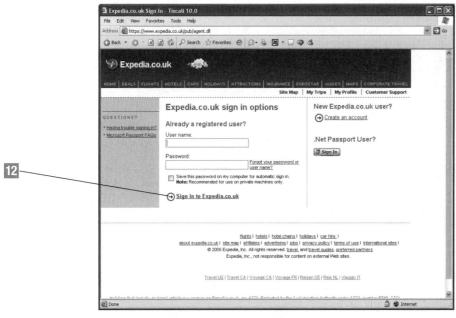

Screenshot from Expedia.co.uk (www.expedia.co.uk).

12 Fill in your log-in details, then click on the Sign in to Expedia.co.uk link.

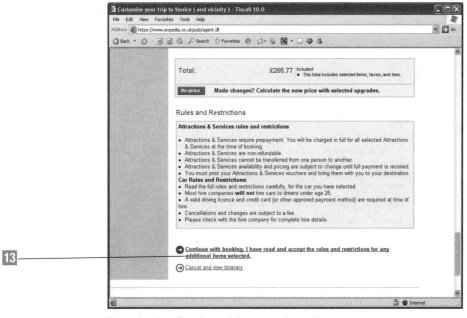

Screenshot from Expedia.co.uk (www.expedia.co.uk).

13 Click on the Continue with booking link.

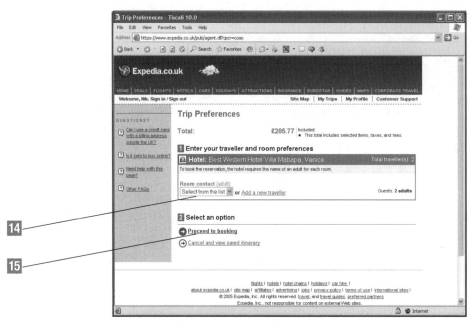

Screenshot from Expedia.co.uk (www.expedia.co.uk).

14 Click on the Room contact drop-down list and click on the person who will be the contact.

15 Click on the Proceed to booking link.

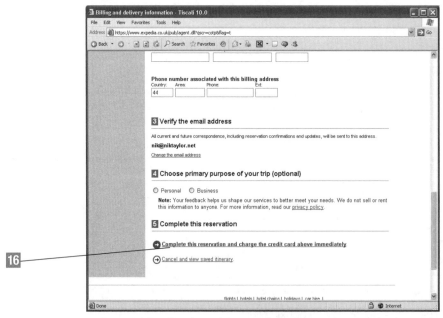

Screenshot from Expedia.co.uk (www.expedia.co.uk).

16 Fill in the final form then click on the Complete this reservation link.

12.4.2 Booking a Hotel on OctopusTravel

By kind permission of octopustravel.com (www.octopustravel.com).

1 Load the OctopusTravel.com site (www.octopustravel.com) in your browser.

2 Fill in the Search for a Hotel form with the details of the hotel stay you want.

3 Click on the Search button.

By kind permission of octopustravel.com (www.octopustravel.com).

4 Click on the Book button next to the hotel you want.

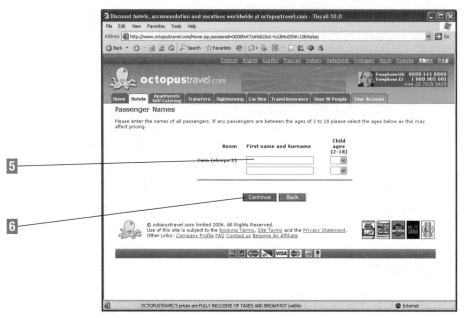

By kind permission of octopustravel.com (www.octopustravel.com).

5 Type in the names of the people staying.

6 Click on the Continue button. If your hotel accepts special requests (such as late check-ins etc.) you'll be asked to choose from these on the next screen. Select the tick boxes of any requests you would like to make, then click Add Request. Now click Continue.

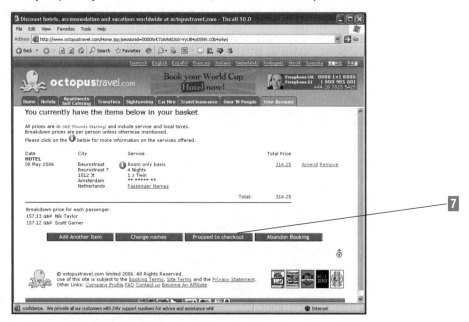

By kind permission of octopustravel.com (www.octopustravel.com).

7 Click the Proceed to Checkout button, then click it again.

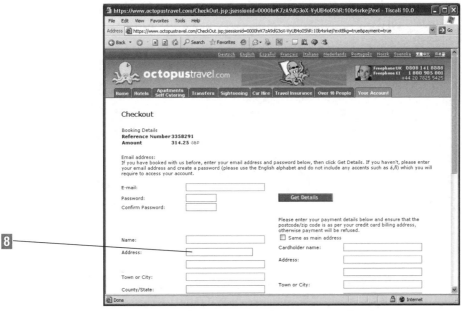

By kind permission of octopustravel.com (www.octopustravel.com).

8 Fill in the form details, then click on the Continue button.

12.5 Hiring a Car

When you need to hire a car, you'll find the whole process is far simpler if you do it online. All the major vehicle hire companies have their own online booking services, so you can go through the whole process using only your computer.

Car rental specialists Hertz have an excellent site from which you can view all the cars available for hire in your location of choice. You can go through the whole rental process using the site, leaving you free to simply turn up and drive off on the day.

12.5.1 Hiring a Car from Hertz

1 Load the Hertz site (www.hertz.co.uk) in your browser.

2 Type where you want to hire the car in the Renting City or Airport Code box.

3 Fill in the dates over which you want to hire the vehicle.

4 Click on the Continue button.

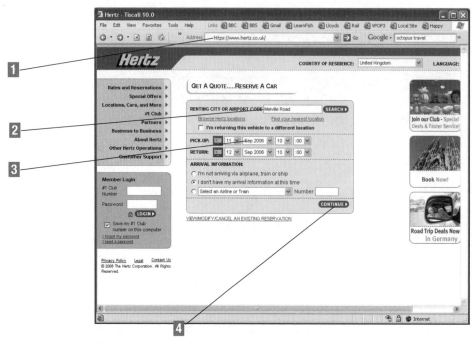

Screenshot from Hertz (www.hertz.co.uk).

5 A pop-up box will appear if you need to clarify your location. Click the links to specify your exact area.

6 Click the button next to the car deal you want. Now click on the continue button.

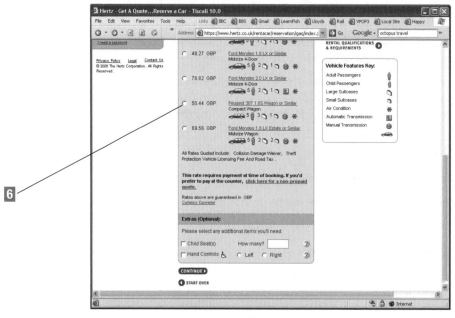

Screenshot from Hertz (www.hertz.co.uk).

7 Fill in the form with your payment details, then click on the Reserve It button.

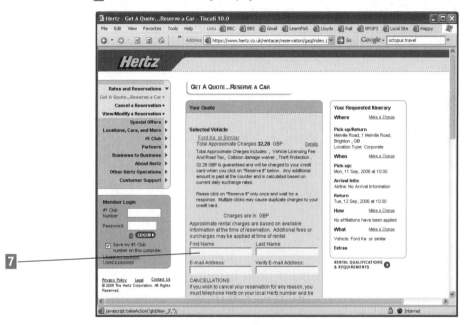

Screenshot from Hertz (www.hertz.co.uk).

12.6 Handy Travel Site Links

Flights

easyJet – www.easyjet.co.uk

Ryanair – www.ryanair.com

Opodo – www.opodo.co.uk (flights)

Virgin Atlantic – www.virgin-atlantic.com

British Airways – www.britishairways.com

Hotels and more

ebookers – www.ebookers.com

Expedia – www.expedia.co.uk

OctopusTravel – www.octopustravel.com

Hotels.com – www.hotels.com

Train times

National Rail Enquiries – www.nationalrail.co.uk

The TrainLine – www.thetrainline.com

Qjump – www.qjump.co.uk

Car hire

Hertz – www.hertz.co.uk

Avis Car Rental – www.avis.co.uk

Thrifty – www.thrifty.co.uk

CHAPTER 13

Learning Online

13.1 Introduction

Now you're getting the hang of finding your way around online, you're probably in the mood for learning more new things. Lucky for you, this is where the Internet excels. You can find information on anything you can think of online, and quite a few things more besides.

Venerable seats of learning such as the Open University have their own websites, where you can search through the course list and even register for a module. University entrance organisation UCAS also has its own place on the Net, enabling would-be students to quickly scan through all the courses offered across the country.

Other sites such as Hotcourses give you the opportunity to scour through thousands of school, college and university courses with just a click of the mouse.

If you want to learn new things without enrolling on a whole course, your local library is the place to go. Many of these now have their own sites, enabling you to search for and reserve books online.

The British Library also has its own website, so you can view many of the items stored there without even getting out of your seat. And if it's books you're after, innovative sites such as Bartleby make old books that are out of copyright available for free.

13.2 Booking Online Courses

Whether you're aiming to take on a full university degree or simply want to start some evening classes at the local college, Hotcourses will be able to help. This free site lists thousands of courses from all over the country which you can quickly search through using the site's search engine. Once you've registered, you can access all the course details and email establishments for further details.

Would-be university students will find the UCAS website fits their needs perfectly. This site enables you to search through all the university courses starting in a particular year, and displays all the links you need in order to apply.

If you want to take a university course, but don't want to give up your day job, take a look at the Open University site. Again, you can search through all the courses available from the institution and even register for some of them online.

13.2.1 Registering with Hotcourses

1 Load the Hotcourses site (www.hotcourses.com) in your browser.

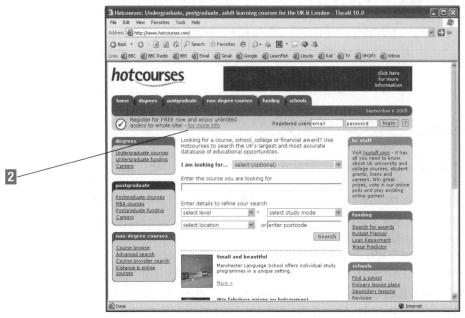

By kind permission of Hotcourses (www.hotcourses.com).

2 Click on the 'for more info' link.

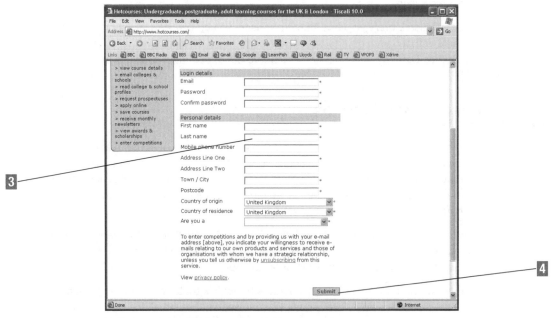

By kind permission of Hotcourses (www.hotcourses.com).

3 Fill in the form.

4 Click on the Submit button.

13.2.2 Emailing About a Course on Hotcourses

1 Load the Hotcourses site (www.hotcourses.com) in your browser.

2 Make sure you are logged into the site (type your details into the Registered users boxes and click on the login button if not).

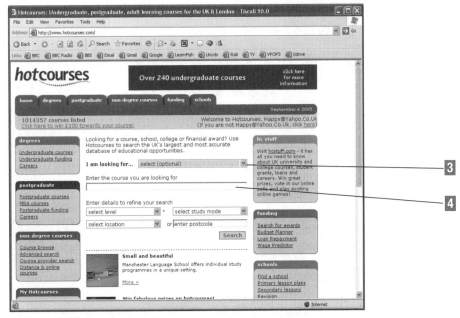

By kind permission of Hotcourses (www.hotcourses.com).

3 Click on the I am looking for... drop-down menu and click on the type of course you want.

4 Fill in the rest of the form, then click on the Search button.

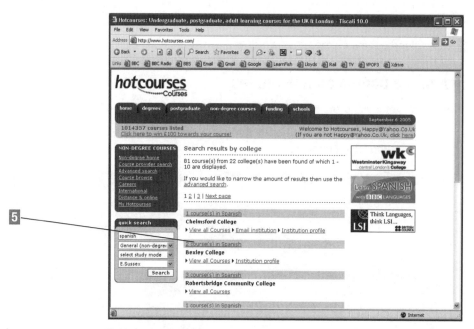

By kind permission of Hotcourses (www.hotcourses.com).

5 Click on the number of courses link for the establishment you're interested in.

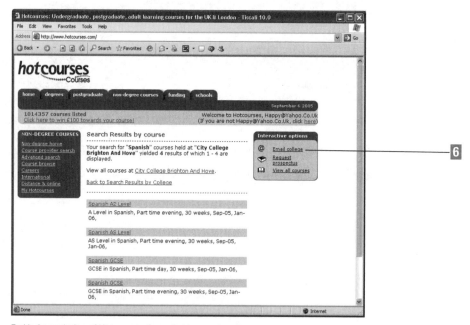

By kind permission of Hotcourses (www.hotcourses.com).

6 Click on the Email college link.

7 Fill in the form, then click on the Send button.

13.2.3 Finding a Course on UCAS

1 Load the UCAS site (www.ucas.ac.uk) in your browser.

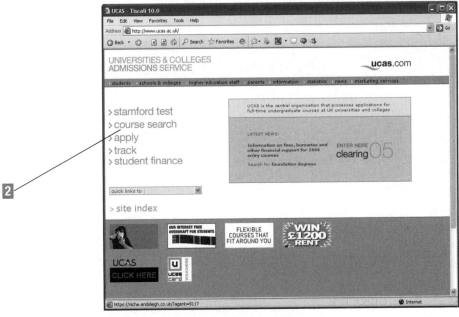

By kind permission of UCAS (www.ucas.ac.uk).

2 Click on the course search link.

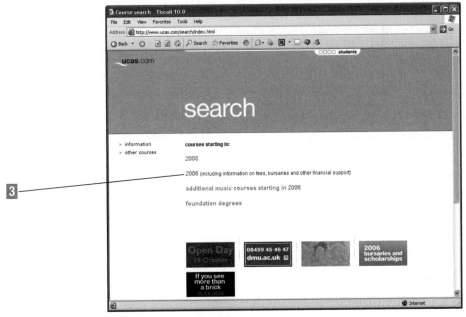

By kind permission of UCAS (www.ucas.ac.uk).

3 Click on the year in which you want the course to start.

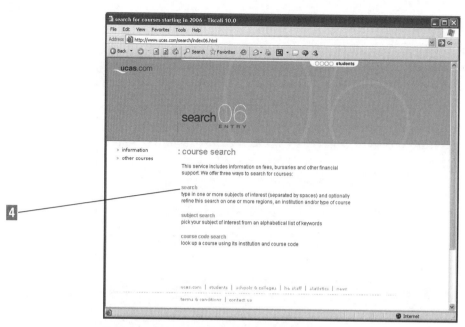

By kind permission of UCAS (www.ucas.ac.uk).

4 Click on the search link.

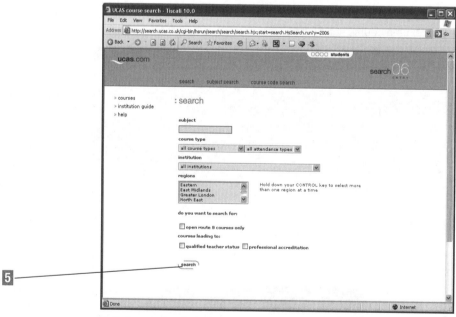

By kind permission of UCAS (www.ucas.ac.uk).

5 Fill in the form, then click on the search link.

13.2.4 Booking a Course on the Open University

1 Load the Open University site (www.open.ac.uk) in your browser.

By kind permission of The Open University (www.open.ac.uk).

2 Click on the Study at the OU link.

3 Click on the subject area you want.

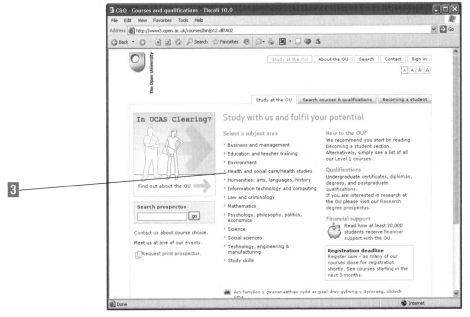

By kind permission of The Open University (www.open.ac.uk).

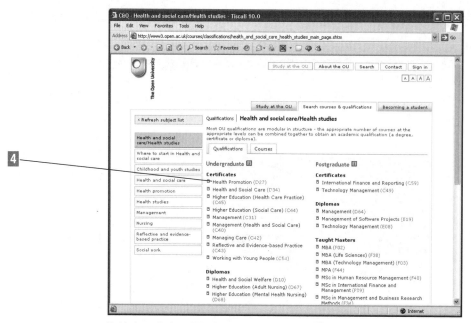

By kind permission of The Open University (www.open.ac.uk).

4 Click on the type of course you want to study.

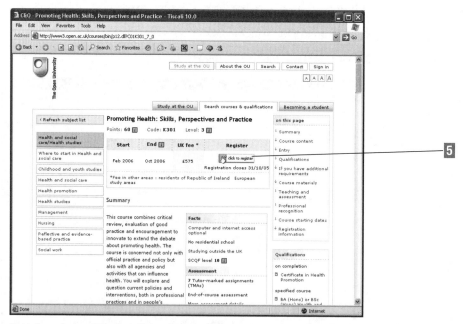

By kind permission of The Open University (www.open.ac.uk).

5 Click on the click to register link (you'll only see this link if you're eligible to take this course).

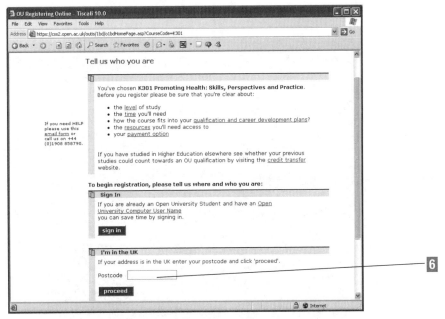

By kind permission of The Open University (www.open.ac.uk).

6 Type in your postcode, then click on the proceed button.

7 Click on your home address, then click on the proceed button.

8 Fill in the forms, clicking on the proceed button each time.

Studying in an online classroom

Online classrooms are simply another form of online training. Students can log on to the classroom site, and be trained no matter where their physical location is. Online classrooms differ from regular online learning because there is a trainer present throughout the lesson, who interacts with the learners.

13.3 Searching Libraries

The Internet is like a huge library in itself, but sometimes there's just no substitute for heading down to your local branch to borrow that important book. However, you no longer need to spend hours searching the shelves in silence, as many libraries are now online. Each library's website will differ slightly, but most will give you the option of searching for and reserving titles from your computer.

The British Library has thousands of rare books and other exhibits, many of which can now be viewed through its website. More than 12 millions items are listed in its catalogue, including newspapers dating back to 1801 and an enormous map section.

13.3.1 Searching the British Library

1 Load the British Library site (www.bl.uk) in your browser.

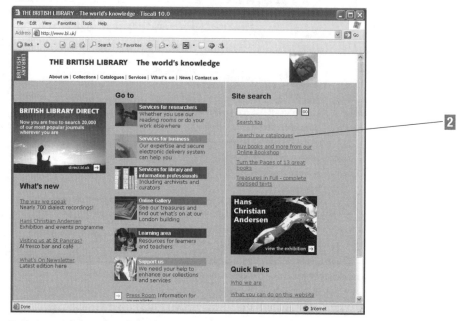

By kind permission of the British Library (www.bl.uk).

2 Click on the Search our catalogues link.

By kind permission of the British Library (www.bl.uk).

3 Click on the Integrated Catalogue link.

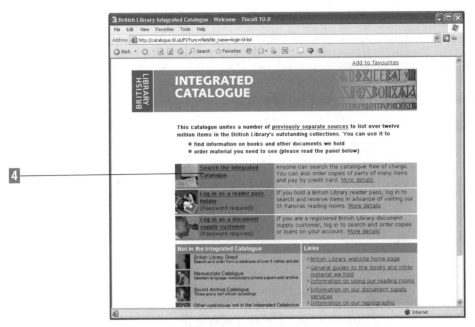

By kind permission of the British Library (www.bl.uk).

4 Click on the Search the Integrated Catalogue link.

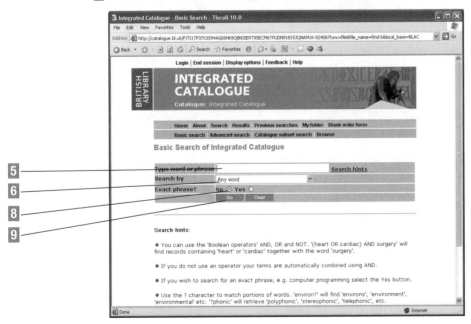

By kind permission of the British Library (www.bl.uk).

5 Type what you want to look for in the Type word or phrase box.

6 Click on the Search by drop-down menu.

7 Click on the type of search you want to make.

8 Click on the relevant button to decide whether to search for the exact phrase or not.

9 Click on the Go button.

13.3.2 Reserving a Book at a Local Library

Different local libraries have different methods of enabling you to make an online reservation. This example shows you how to use the Brighton & Hove reservation system.

1 Load the Brighton & Hove Library (www.librarycatalogue.info) site in your browser.

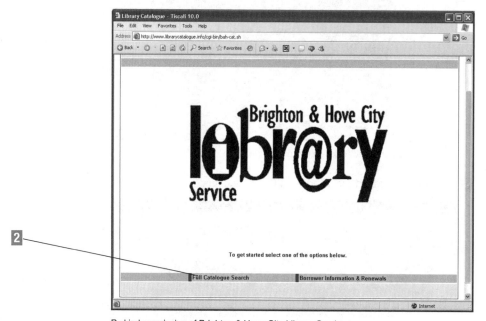

By kind permission of Brighton & Hove City Library Service.

2 Click on the Full Catalogue Search button.

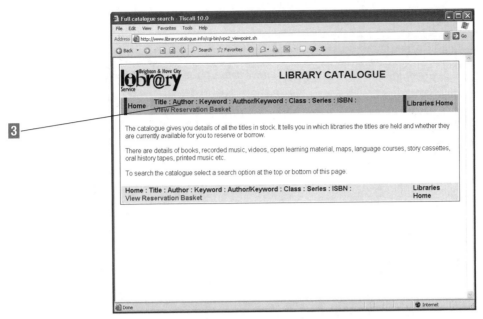

By kind permission of Brighton & Hove City Library Service.

3 Click on the link for the type of search you want to make (by author, title, etc.)

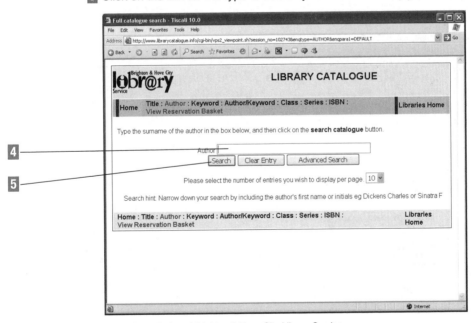

By kind permission of Brighton & Hove City Library Service.

4 Type in a search keyword.

5 Click on the Search button.

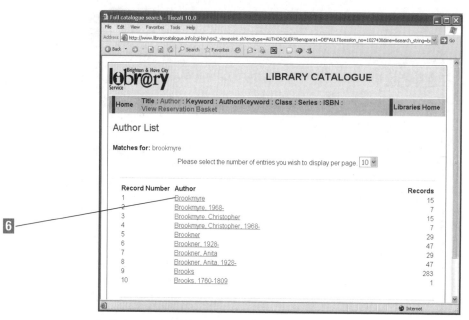

By kind permission of Brighton & Hove City Library Service.

6 Click on the link for the item/author that matches your search.

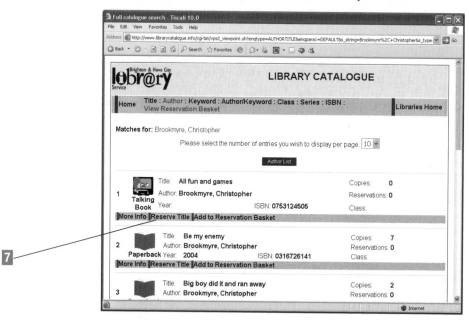

By kind permission of Brighton & Hove City Library Service.

7 Click on the Reserve Title link beneath the name of the book you want.

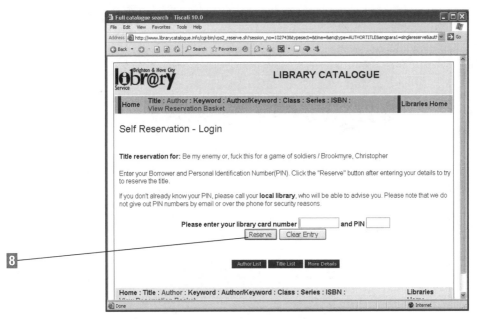

By kind permission of Brighton & Hove City Library Service.

8 Type in your library log-in details, then click on the Reserve button.

13.4 Finding Books Online

Proving that you really can get something for nothing is the intriguing Bartleby site. Named after the main character from Herman Melville's short story *Bartleby, the Scrivener* (Melville also wrote the somewhat more celebrated Moby Dick), a trip to this site enables you to read thousands of books for free.

Bartleby is able to offer this service as everything it publishes is out of copyright. So, a wide range of works of literature, non-fiction and reference can be read on the site or printed out to read later.

13.4.1 Downloading Free Books from Bartleby

1 Open the Bartleby (www.bartleby.com) site in your browser.

2 Click on the drop-down menu for the type of book you want.

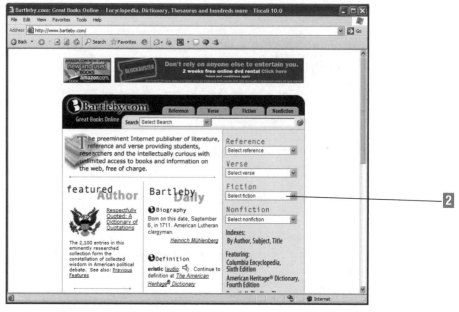

By kind permission of Bartleby.com (www.bartleby.com).

3 Click on the book or author you want from the list.

4 If you selected an author, click on the title you want to view.

5 Click on the link for the section of the book you want to view.

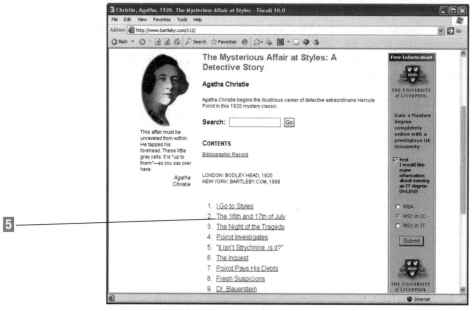

By kind permission of Bartleby.com (www.bartleby.com).

6 Scroll down the page to read the text.

13.5 Handy Learning Site Links

Courses

Hotcourses – www.hotcourses.com

Open University – www.open.ac.uk

UCAS – www.ucas.com

Libraries

Oxford University Libraries – www.lib.ox.ac.uk

British Library – www.bl.uk

Cambridge University Library – www.lib.cam.ac.uk

National Library of Scotland – www.nls.uk

National Library of Wales – www.llgc.org.uk

Free books

The Online Books Page – http://onlinebooks.library.upenn.edu

Project Gutenberg – www.gutenberg.org

Bartleby – www.bartleby.com

13

CHAPTER 14

Job Hunting

14.1 Introduction

Fancy earning a bit more money? Had enough of squeezing onto packed trains for your daily commute? Or are you sick and tired of the bad habits of the person at the desk next to you? Well, you need a new job, and fast. And the easiest way to bag one is to join the hordes of people now using the net for job-hunting.

Forget about tedious hours spent poring over the small ads in your local paper – going online can save you huge amounts of time and effort. Open any of the major job sites in your browser and you can instantly run a search for the new career you're after. Tap in a couple of keywords and all the matching vacancies will pop onto your screen, along with all the details you need.

Even better, you can refine your search by using the advanced features. That means you can specify where in the country you would like to work, or set a salary level you're prepared to accept. Then, once you've found a job you like the look of, you can complete an application from your computer.

To make the whole process even easier, you can store your CV online so it can be instantly attached to your online application. If you wish, you can make this visible to potential employers so they can search your CV whenever they're looking for a new employee.

In addition, there are loads of sites on which you can find tips on applying for jobs, as well as advice on your rights in the workplace.

14.2 Searching for Jobs

14

Using a job site to search for work is just as straightforward as using a search engine. All you need to do is tap in a couple of keywords that describe the type of job you're after. Run the search and the site will instantly display any matching vacancies it has listed. Once you've dug up something likely-looking, clicking on the job title will bring up all the details on how to apply.

14.2.1 Searching Monster.co.uk for Jobs

By kind permission of Monster (www.monster.co.uk).

1 Open the Monster site (www.monster.co.uk) in your browser.

2 Click in the Keyword box and type in the type of job you're after.

3 Click on the Job Category drop-down menu and choose the relevant category

4 Click on the Location drop-down menu and click on the location you want.

5 Click on the Search Jobs button.

6 Click on a job title to find out more.

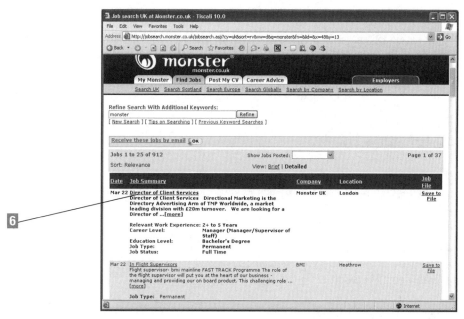

By kind permission of Monster (www.monster.co.uk).

14.2.2 Applying for a Job on Monster

1 Run a job search on www.monster.co.uk as normal.

2 Click on the job title you want to apply for.

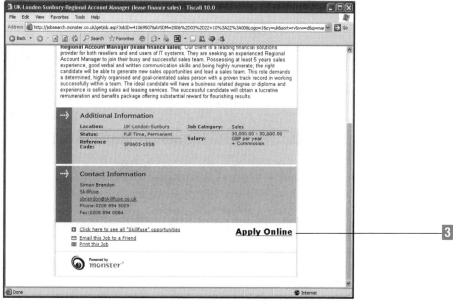

By kind permission of Monster (www.monster.co.uk).

3 Look for a link that will enable you to apply online, then click there.

14.3 Applying for Jobs Online

Fish4 is another gargantuan jobs site, covering vacancies across the whole of the UK. It works in pretty much the same way as Monster – just type in a couple of words that describe the job you're after, then click on the titles of the positions you want to find out more about.

Many of the adverts you'll find here include the option to apply for the job online. To do this, you first need to make sure you have a copy of your CV saved on your hard drive (preferably as a Microsoft Word file).

14.3.1 Applying for a Job on Fish4

1 Open the Fish4 Jobs site (www.fish4jobs.co.uk) in your browser.

By kind permission of Fish4 Trading Ltd (www.fish4.co.uk).

2 Type the job you're after into the Job title box.

3 Use the Within boxes to specify a location.

4 Click on the search button.

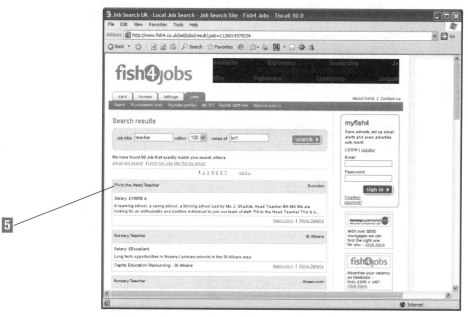

By kind permission of Fish4 Trading Ltd (www.fish4.co.uk).

5 Click on a job's title to read more information about it.

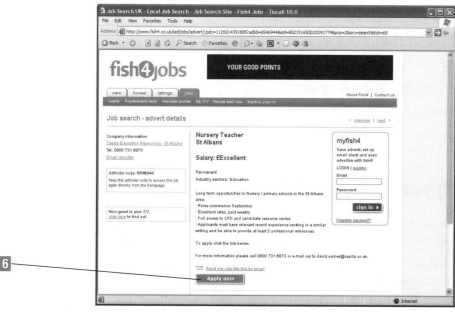

By kind permission of Fish4 Trading Ltd (www.fish4.co.uk).

6 Click on the Apply now button to apply.

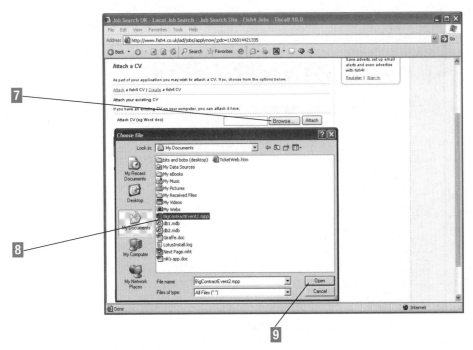

By kind permission of Fish4 Trading Ltd (www.fish4.co.uk).

7 Click on the Browse button.

8 Select your CV file from your hard drive.

9 Click on the Open button.

10 Click on the Attach button.

11 Fill in the rest of the form.

12 Click on the Submit button.

14.4 Posting your CV on the Net

As well as the usual career-searching features, Monster also includes the option to save your CV onto your account. This is useful for a couple of reasons.

First, you can store the CV there so it's easier to access whenever you want to apply for a job on the site.

Second, you can choose to make it searchable. That means, whenever an employer runs a search for people on the site, your details will pop up if they match the search being made. You could end up being offered your dream job without even knowing it was up for grabs!

14.4.1 Adding your CV to Monster

By kind permission of Monster (www.monster.co.uk).

1 Load the Monster site (www.monster.co.uk) in your browser.

2 Click on the Post My CV link.

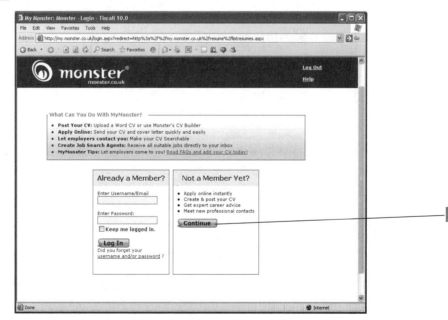

By kind permission of Monster (www.monster.co.uk).

3 Click on the Continue button.

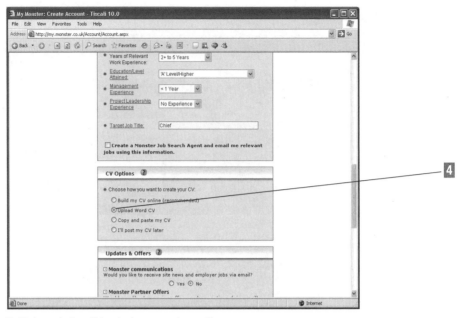

By kind permission of Monster (www.monster.co.uk).

4 Fill in the form, making sure you click on the Upload Word CV button.

5 Click on the Create Account button.

6 Fill in the form.

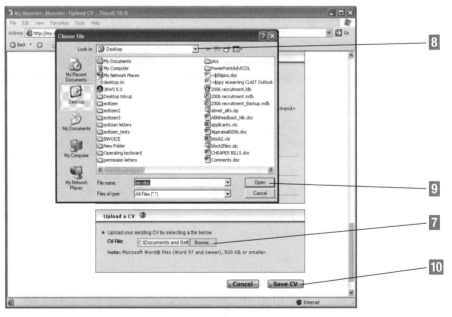

By kind permission of Monster (www.monster.co.uk).

7 Click on the Browse button in the Upload a CV section.

8 Click on the Look in box, then select the file you want to attach.

9 Click on the Open button.

10 Click on the Save CV button.

14.5 Finding Tips on Applying for Jobs

If job interviews are proving a little hard to come by, or you're making lots of applications but not really getting anywhere, you might benefit from a different approach when putting yourself forward for jobs.

For instance, you could overhaul your CV to make it more applicable to the jobs you're going for. Or you could make some changes to how your cover letters are penned. There are plenty of ways to make your application stand out from the crowd, and we could all do with a little helping hand when it comes to job hunting.

There's lots of advice on the Internet on how to spice up your applications. Monster includes a compact but useful section of career tips.

14.5.1 Help on Applying

By kind permission of Monster (www.monster.co.uk).

1 Open the Monster site (www.monster.co.uk) in your browser.

2 Click on the Career Advice link.

3

By kind permission of Monster (www.monster.co.uk).

3 Click on the appropriate links to get more help on applying for jobs.

14.6 Checking Employment Issues

Got a work-related question that you're not comfortable bringing up around the office? A quick scoot around the Net can give you all the information you need about employment laws and regulations.

Government sites are very thorough and will probably cover all you need to know – or offer you links to where you can find the advice you need. You can also order leaflets and guides for all sorts of employment issues, such as pensions.

14.6.1 Employment Advice from Directgov

1 Open the Directgov site (www.directgov.gov.uk) in your browser.

2 Click on the Employees & Work link.

3 Click on the relevant links to find the advice you need.

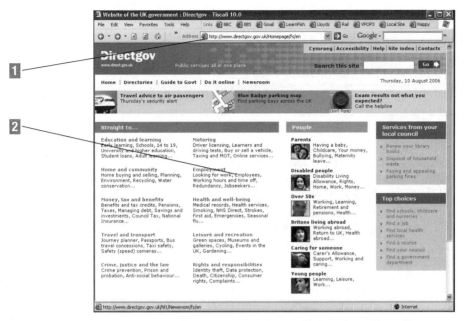

Crown copyright of the Department for Trade and Industry (www.dti.gov.uk).

Crown copyright of the Department for Trade and Industry (www.dti.gov.uk).

14.6.2 Requesting Pension Advice from the Government

1 Open The Pension Service site (www.thepensionservice.gov.uk) in your browser.

2 Click on the Resource centre link.

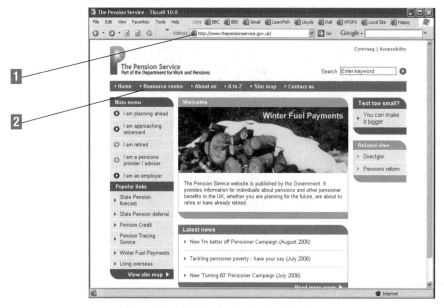

Crown copyright of the Pension Service (http://thepensionservice.gov.uk).

3 Click on Guides and forms.

4 Click on the type of guide you need.

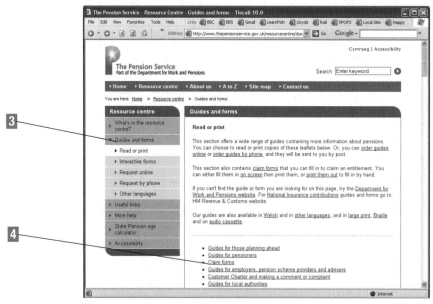

Crown copyright of the Pension Service (http://thepensionservice.gov.uk).

5 Click on the title of a guide to read it as a PDF.

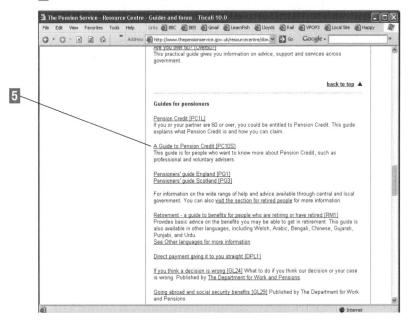

Crown copyright of the Pension Service (http://thepensionservice.gov.uk).

Ordering guides to be delivered

Follow the first three steps above, then scroll to the top of the page. Click on the Order guides online link, then fill out the following form to have the guides delivered to you.

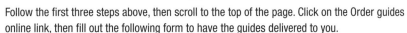

14.7 | Handy Job Site Links

Job-hunting

The Guardian Jobs – http://jobs.guardian.co.uk

Monster.co.uk – www.monster.co.uk

Fish4 Jobs – www.fish4jobs.co.uk

Total Jobs.com – www.totaljobs.com

Jobsite – www.jobsite.co.uk

Work issues

DTI – www.dti.gov.uk

The Pension Service – www.thepensionservice.gov.uk

Health and Safety Executive – www.hse.gov.uk

14

CHAPTER 15

Health Information

15.1 Introduction

The web is heaving with pages offering health advice, but you should be cautious with these. When taking advice on something as serious as your own health, you need to be doubly sure the site you're using is trustworthy and accurate.

If you've got a concern about your health or that of someone you know, the best place to go is the NHS Direct website. On there you can complete a simple health check to find out what your symptoms may mean, or you can complete an online query. Of course, if you're really concerned then this is no substitute for a visit to your doctor, but it can be a useful port of call.

Should you decide you want to look into private healthcare, you'll find plenty of options online. The BUPA website has a fully searchable directory of all its establishments, as well as details of its pricing. You'll be able to find many more private healthcare companies by running a simple search on a search engine.

Similarly, there are many sites offering information on alternative healthcare. One of the best is CHIS-UK. This has an excellent directory section, which you can use to find practitioners of any type of alternative therapy in your area.

As health providers become more established on the web, so the number of services available continues to increase. One example is the Choose and Book system being phased in by the NHS. Once this is fully operational, it will enable hospital outpatients to go online to select their own appointment times, rather than being given a time that may be inconvenient.

15.2 Checking Symptoms with NHS Direct

The main idea of the NHS Direct site is to make it easier for people to know what to do if they or someone close to them is feeling unwell. Using the site, you can quickly check up what common symptoms may indicate, so you can get a decent idea of whether a trip to the local GP is required.

If you need further advice, you can get in touch with the NHS Direct team of nurses, either by email or over the telephone.

15.2.1 Checking your Symptoms

1 Load the NHS Direct (www.nhsdirect.nhs.uk) site in your browser.

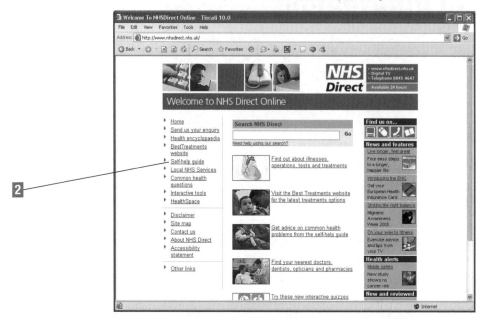

Crown copyright of NHS Direct (www.nhsdirect.nhs.uk).

2 Click on the Self-help guide link.

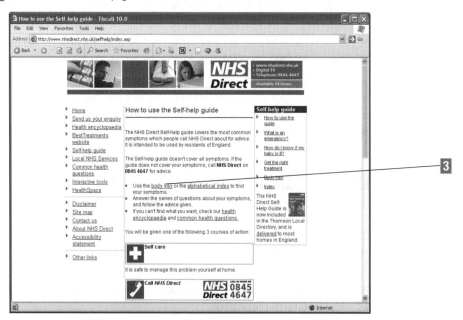

Crown copyright of NHS Direct (www.nhsdirect.nhs.uk).

3 Click on the Body key link.

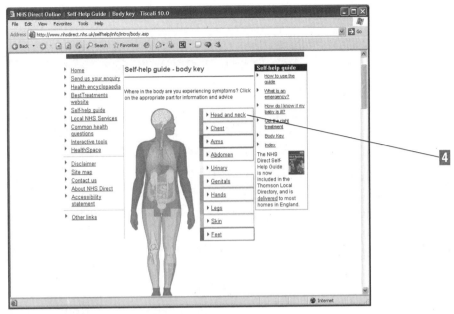

Crown copyright of NHS Direct (www.nhsdirect.nhs.uk).

4 Click on the area where the symptoms are.

5 Click on the type of symptom.

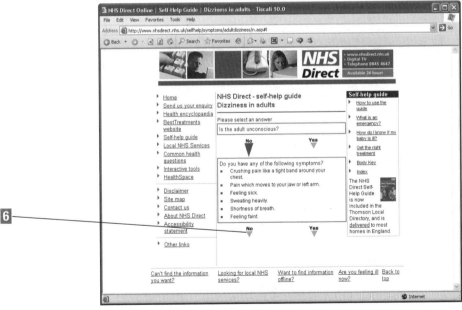

Crown copyright of NHS Direct (www.nhsdirect.nhs.uk).

6 Click on the relevant links to go through the diagnosis.

15.2.2 Emailing a Health Enquiry

1 Load the NHS Direct (www.nhsdirect.nhs.uk) site in your browser.

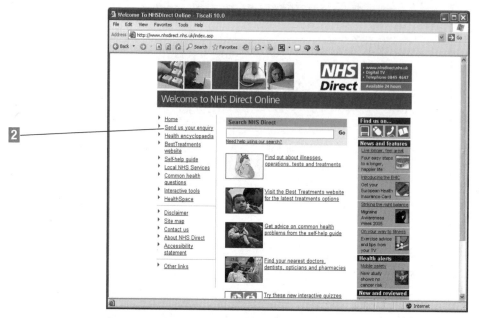

Crown copyright of NHS Direct (www.nhsdirect.nhs.uk).

2 Click on the Send us your enquiry link.

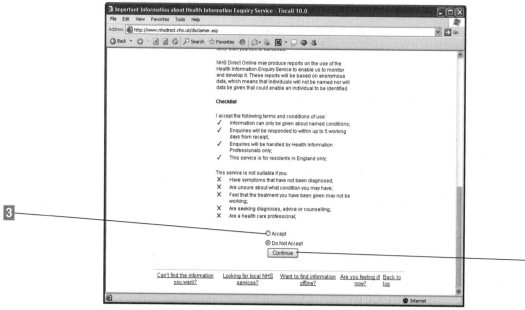

Crown copyright of NHS Direct (www.nhsdirect.nhs.uk).

3 Read the terms, then click on the Accept button.

4 Click on the Continue button.

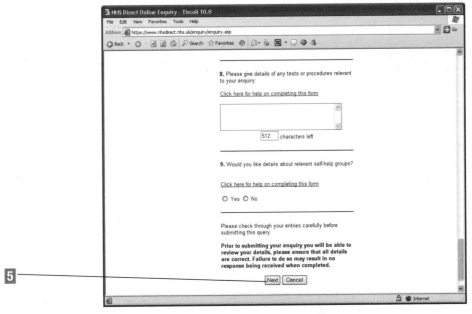

Crown copyright of NHS Direct (www.nhsdirect.nhs.uk).

5 Fill in the form, then click on the Next button.

6 Click on the Send Enquiry button to send the email (or click on Go Back to amend any of the details you've entered).

Having form trouble?

If you have difficulty filling out any sections of the form, click on the 'Click here for help on completing this form' link which you'll see in each section.

15.3 Finding Private Healthcare

Nobody likes to be stuck in a queue, so if you want to skip the NHS waiting lists then going private is the way forward. Running a search for 'private healthcare' will bring up plenty of online options for you – but BUPA is one of the best known.

BUPA has a well-presented, easy-to-use website that will give you all the info you need on signing up health insurance. A built-in search engine makes it simple to find a BUPA facility near you, and all the prices are listed here too.

15

15.3.1 Finding a BUPA Hospital

1 Open the BUPA site (www.bupa.co.uk) in your browser.

By kind permission of BUPA (www.bupa.co.uk).

2 Click on the facilities finder link.

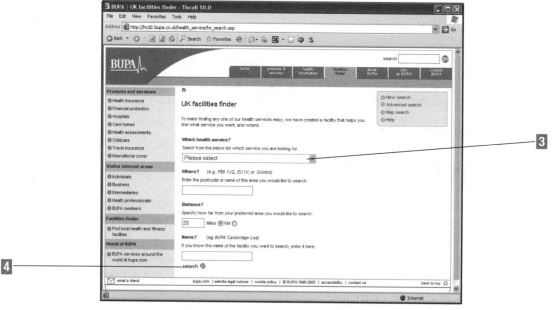

By kind permission of BUPA (www.bupa.co.uk).

3 Fill in the form with the details of the service you want to find.

4 Click on the Search button.

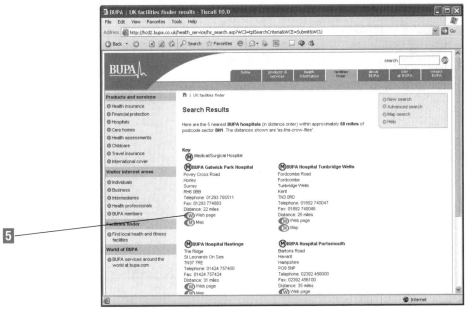

By kind permission of BUPA (www.bupa.co.uk).

5 Click on the Web page link for the hospital whose details you want to see.

15.3.2 Checking BUPA Insurance Options

1 Open the BUPA site (www.bupa.co.uk) in your browser.

2 Click on the Health insurance link.

3 Click on the Health care select 1–4 link.

4 Click on the PDF option for the healthcare you want to find out about.

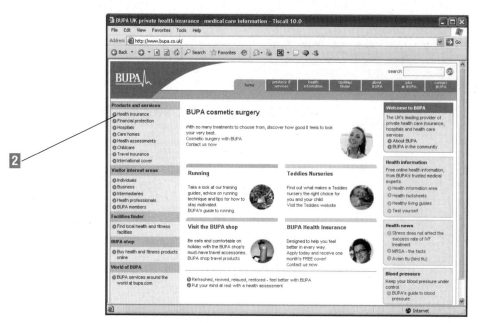

By kind permission of BUPA (www.bupa.co.uk).

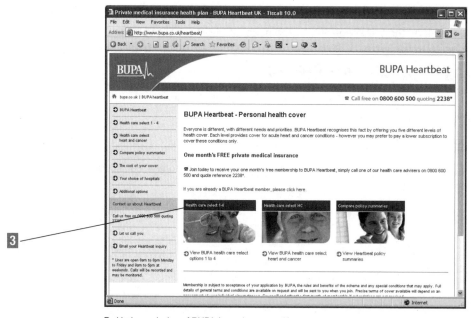

By kind permission of BUPA (www.bupa.co.uk).

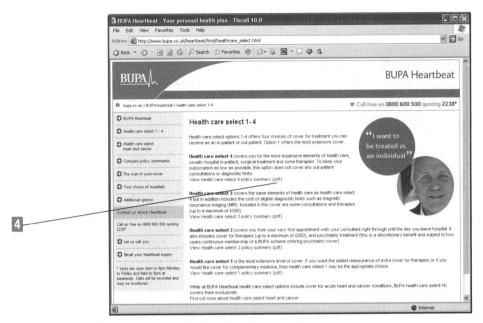

By kind permission of BUPA (www.bupa.co.uk).

15.4 Finding Alternative Healthcare Practitioners

Alternative healthcare isn't all about sitting cross-legged in a cave, surrounded by healing crystals and going 'ohhhhmmm' a lot. But then you probably knew that.

These days complementary medicine has shaken off its hippy-dippy image, and the proven health benefits of therapies such as acupuncture, hypnotherapy and reflexology attract legions of devotees.

There are lots of alternative healthcare sites out there, but CHIS-UK stands out because of its excellent directory section. Using this you can find a relevant therapist who is close to where you live.

15.4.1 Finding an Alternative Health Practice

1 Load the CHIS-UK site (www.chisuk.org.uk) in your browser.

2 Click on the Directories link.

3 Click on the Search all regions drop-down menu.

4 Click on the region in which you want to search.

5 Click on the Submit your search button.

6 Click on the Choose a therapy drop-down menu.

7 Click on the therapy you want to search for.

By kind permission of CHIS-UK (www.chisuk.org.uk).

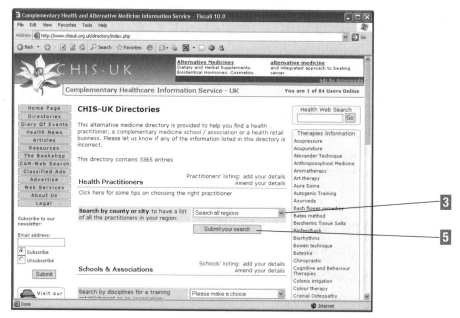

By kind permission of CHIS-UK (www.chisuk.org.uk).

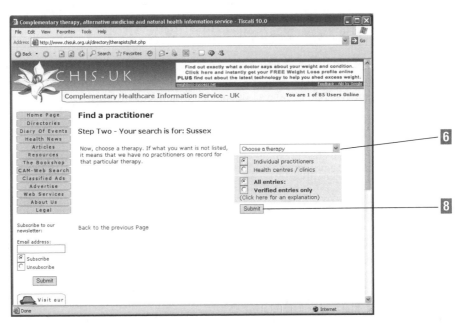

By kind permission of CHIS-UK (www.chisuk.org.uk).

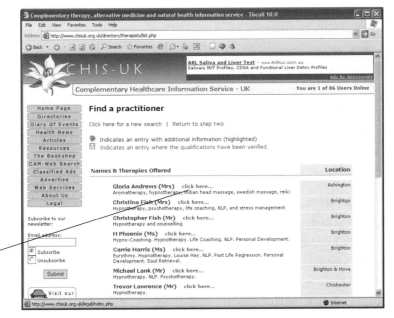

By kind permission of CHIS-UK (www.chisuk.org.uk).

8 Click on the Submit button.

9 Click on the name of the practice you're interested in to see its details.

15.5 | Choosing your Own Appointment Time

The Internet is all about making things easier, and even the National Health Service is getting in on the act. The Choose and Book system is still being developed at the moment, and has had a few well-documented problems already.

However, once it's up and running, the service will make getting a hospital appointment much less of a trial. Instead of being given a time and date that may not be suitable, patients will be able to go online and select the appointment time that suits them best. You can find out more about the service by visiting the site.

15.5.1 Finding out More About Choose and Book

1 Load the Choose and Book (www.chooseandbook.nhs.uk) site in your browser.

2 Click on the links to find out more about the service.

15.6 | Handy Health Site Links

NHS sites

NHS Direct – www.nhsdirect.nhs.uk

NHS England – www.nhs.uk

NHS Wales – www.wales.nhs.uk

NHS Scotland – www.show.scot.nhs.uk

Health and Care Northern Ireland – www.n-i.nhs.uk

Givingupsmoking – www.givingupsmoking.co.uk

Department of Health – www.dh.gov.uk

Private healthcare

Private Healthcare UK – www.privatehealth.co.uk

BUPA – www.bupa.co.uk

Nuffield Hospitals – www.nuffieldhospitals.org.uk

BMI Healthcare – www.bmihealthcare.co.uk

Complementary medicine

BCMA – www.bcma.co.uk

CHIS-UK – www.chisuk.org.uk

CHAPTER 16

Online Communities

16.1 | Introduction

Millions upon millions of people from all over the world have access to the Internet – which makes it possible for any of them to communicate with each other instantly.

There are many ways people can have a chat online, including email, instant messaging and even the option to make free phone calls via the Internet.

But one of the oldest methods of communicating online – and one that's still going strong – is via something known as a 'newsgroup'.

Newsgroups are basically online discussion groups where people can chat about their interests. Each newsgroup is dedicated to a particular subject, and there are thousands of them on the web.

It used to be that you had to have specialist software in order to read the messages in a newsgroup, but not any more. Newsgroups are now fully integrated within the web, so you can read through them by simply visiting a web page.

These groups work in a fairly straightforward way. Users can post up a message about whatever they want to talk about, and everyone else can then read these messages and reply to them if they want. The result is that you get long text-based discussions, to which anyone can add their point of view.

Another example of an 'online community' is a message board. These sites work in basically the same way as newsgroups. The main difference from a user's perspective is simply that they look a bit smarter and include more advanced options. For instance, when you post a reply you can also attach files, such as pictures.

While we're on the subject of getting in touch with people, being on the web makes it easier to get involved in your local community as well. Several sites list voluntary work that can be found in your local area, and all the major charities have their own websites on which you can apply to become a volunteer.

16

16.2 Finding Voluntary Work

Want to make a difference to your local community? A quick click around the Net will uncover several sites listing volunteering opportunities all over the UK. Keep an eye on these sites and you'll soon find something within your local area.

Another option is to go straight to the home page of your favourite charity. Most charities will include a page that lists their current volunteering vacancies as well as details on how to put yourself forward.

16.2.1 Volunteering your Time

1 Load the Volunteering England (http://volunteering.org.uk) site in your browser.

By kind permission of the Volunteering England website (www.volunteering.org.uk).

2 Click on the I want to volunteer link.

3 Click on the link entitled Find out about volunteering in you area.

4 Click on your county on the map.

5 Click on the website link for the volunteering organisation you're interested in.

By kind permission of the Volunteering England website (www.volunteering.org.uk).

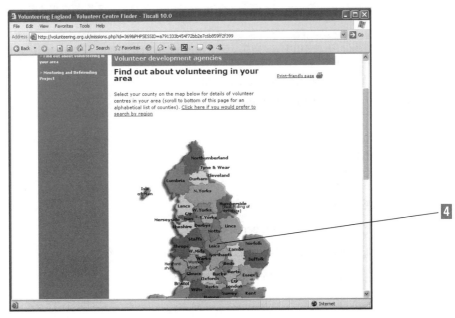

By kind permission of the Volunteering England website (www.volunteering.org.uk).

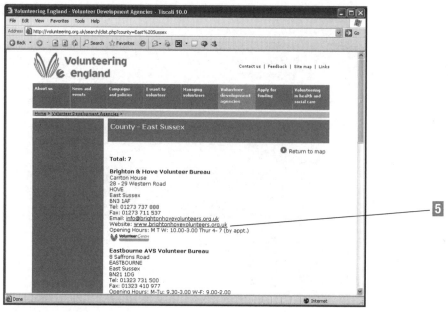

By kind permission of the Volunteering England website (www.volunteering.org.uk).

Don't live in England?

Try these sites…

Scotland: www.volunteerscotland.info

Wales: www.volunteering-wales.net

Northern Ireland: www.volunteering-ni.org

16.2.2 Working for a Charity

1 Load the Oxfam site (www.oxfam.co.uk) in your browser.

2 Click on the Jobs at Oxfam link.

3 Click on the Volunteer at Oxfam link.

4 Click on the Latest opportunities link.

5 Click on the job title you fancy.

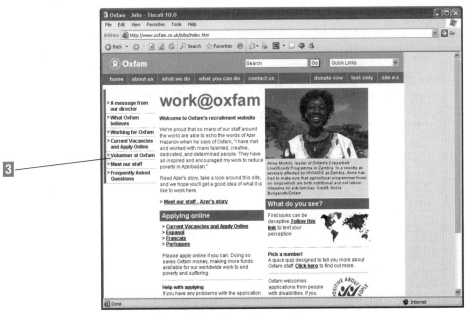

By kind permission of Oxfam (www.oxfam.co.uk).

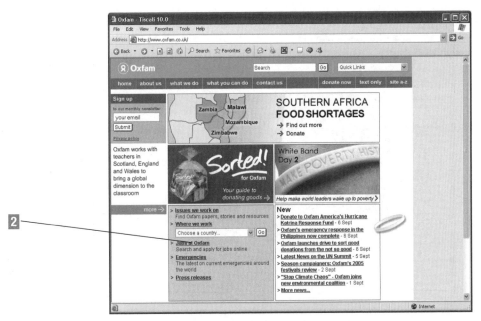

By kind permission of Oxfam (www.oxfam.co.uk).

By kind permission of Oxfam (www.oxfam.co.uk).

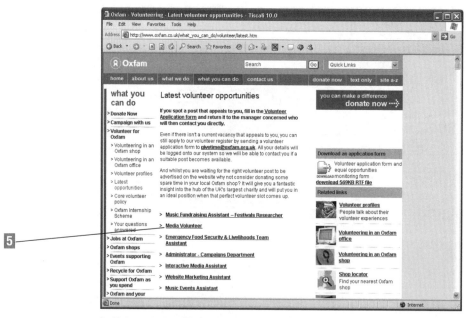

By kind permission of Oxfam (www.oxfam.co.uk).

16.3 | Newsgroups

Newsgroups, also known as discussion groups, consist of messages posted on a particular subject. There are newsgroups out there for pretty much every subject you can think of – and if you can't find a group on your interests, you can create your own.

It used to be that you needed specialist software known as a 'newsreader' in order to read the messages on a newsgroup. That's no longer the case. The easiest way to read and post on newsgroups is to go to the Google Groups site, from where you can search through all the postings made.

16.3.1 Browsing Newsgroups

1 Open the Google Groups (http://groups.google.co.uk) site in your browser.

By kind permission of Google (www.google.co.uk).

2 Type a search term in the Find a group box.

3 Click on the Search for a group button.

4 Click on a sub-topic if you want to refine your search further.

5 Click on the green link for the newsgroup you want to read.

6 Click on the message you want to read.

7 To instead search all newsgroups for a particular phrase, type the search terms into the box at the top then click on the search button.

8 Click on the message you want to read.

16

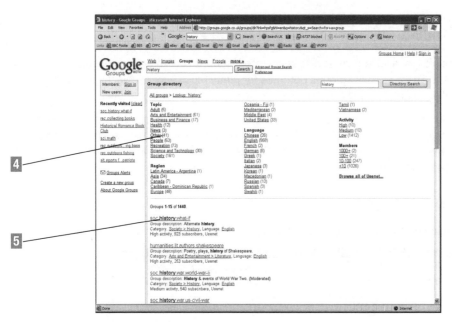

By kind permission of Google (www.google.co.uk).

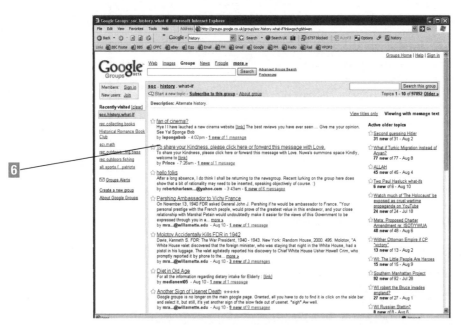

By kind permission of Google (www.google.co.uk).

By kind permission of Google (www.google.co.uk).

16.3.2 Joining a Members Only Newsgroup

Some newsgroups require you to become a member before you can post any messages yourself.

1 Open the Google Groups (http://groups.google.co.uk) site in your browser.

By kind permission of Google (www.google.co.uk).

2 Type a search term in the Find a group box.

3 Click on the Search for a group button.

By kind permission of Google (www.google.co.uk).

4 Click on a sub-topic if you want to refine your search further.

5 Click on a members-only group (these are the ones that are listed as 'restricted').

By kind permission of Google (www.google.co.uk).

6 Click on the Join this group link.

By kind permission of Google (www.google.co.uk).

7 Click on the Sign up now link.

8 Fill in the form, then click on the Create my account button.

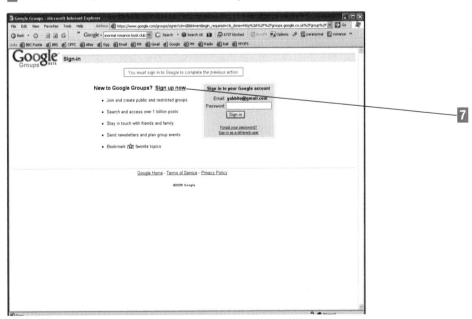

By kind permission of Google (www.google.co.uk).

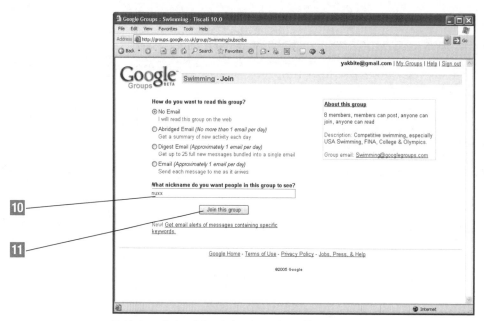

By kind permission of Google (www.google.co.uk).

9 Click on the activation link in the email you'll receive from Google (a new window will open).

10 Type in a nickname for yourself if required.

11 Click on the Join this group button.

16.3.3 Posting a Message on a Newsgroup

1 Open the Google Groups (http://groups.google.co.uk) site in your browser.

2 Open a newsgroup you're interested in.

3 Click on the more link of a message you're interested in.

4 Click on the Reply link.

5 Type your reply.

6 Click on the Post message button.

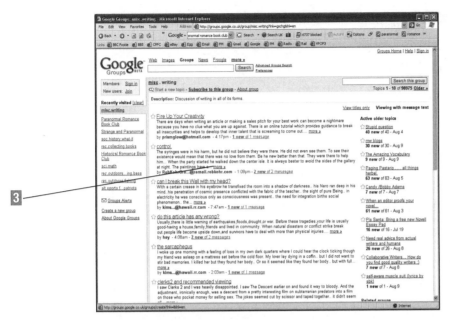

By kind permission of Google (www.google.co.uk).

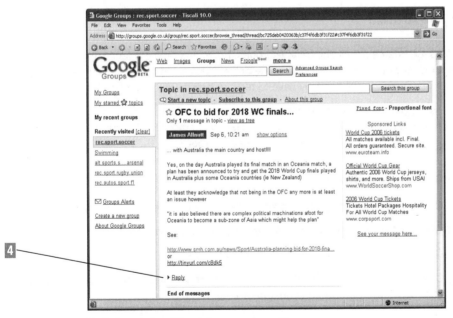

By kind permission of Google (www.google.co.uk).

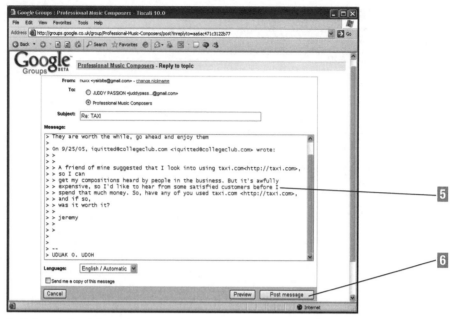

By kind permission of Google (www.google.co.uk).

16.4 Message Boards

Message boards are similar to newsgroups, but with a bit more fancy formatting. The idea of a message board is that it's full of separate discussions, to which anyone can post their own responses. You'll normally have to register before you can post on a message board.

Message boards are generally devoted to a single subject, such as films, or a particular football team. The BBC site has a large collection of message boards, so a visit there is sure to find one on a subject you fancy chatting about.

16.4.1 Viewing a Message Board

1 Open the BBC message boards site (www.bbc.co.uk/messageboards) in your browser.

2 Click on the button for the type of message board you want to view.

3 Click on the message board name you're interested in.

4 Click on the title of the discussion you want to read (you can see how many replies each discussion has in the column next to its title).

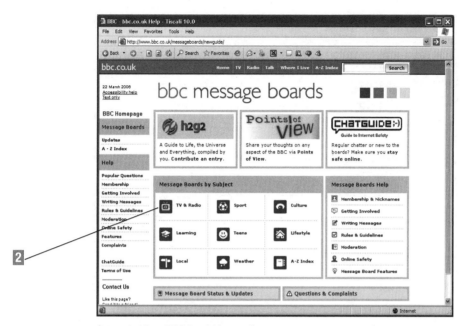

Screenshot from BBC (www.bbc.co.uk).

Screenshot from BBC (www.bbc.co.uk).

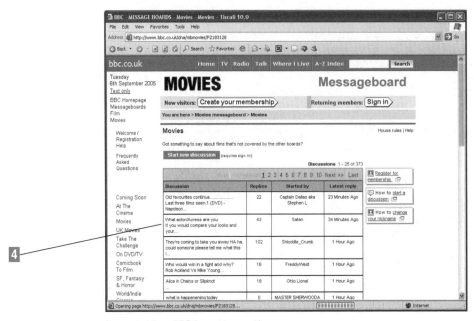

Screenshot from BBC (www.bbc.co.uk).

16.4.2 Joining a Message Board

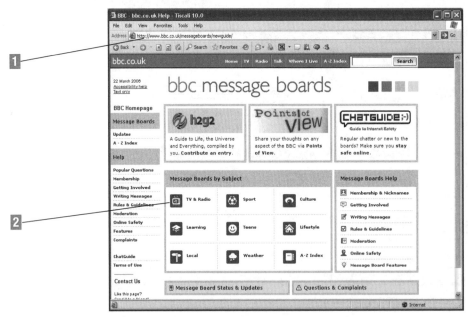

Screenshot from BBC (www.bbc.co.uk).

1 Open the BBC message boards site (www.bbc.co.uk/messageboards) in your browser.

2 Click on the type of message board you want to view.

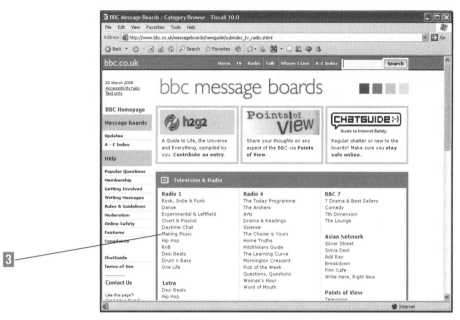

Screenshot from BBC (www.bbc.co.uk).

3 Click on the message board name you're interested in.

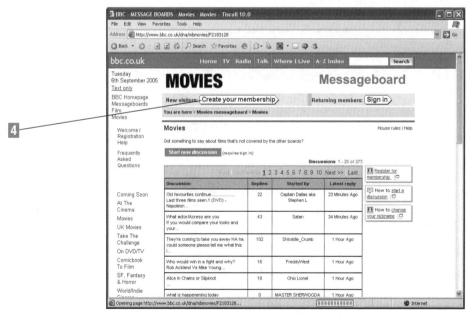

Screenshot from BBC (www.bbc.co.uk).

4 Click on the Create your membership link.

5 Follow the step-by-step process to join up.

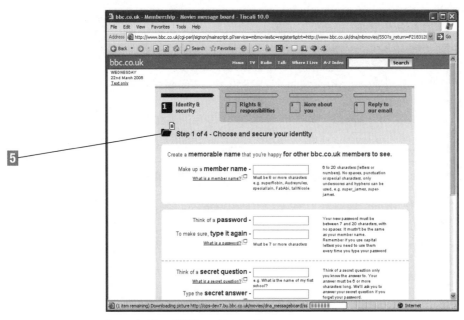

Screenshot from BBC (www.bbc.co.uk).

16.4.3 Posting on a Message Board

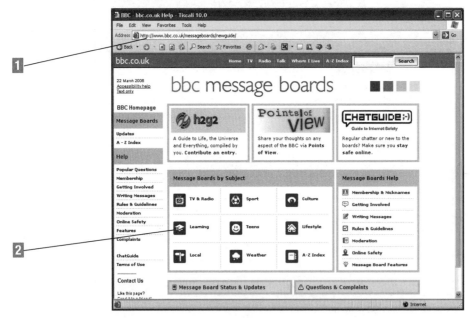

Screenshot from BBC (www.bbc.co.uk).

1 Open the BBC message boards site (www.bbc.co.uk/messageboards) in your browser.

2 Click on the type of message board you want to view.

Screenshot from BBC (www.bbc.co.uk).

3 Click on the message board name you're interested in.

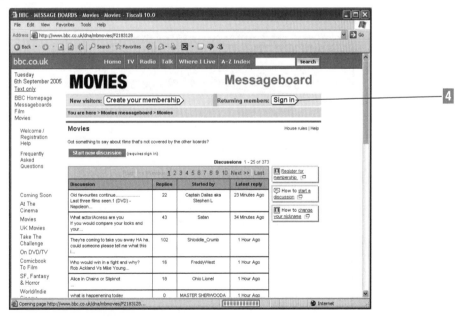

Screenshot from BBC (www.bbc.co.uk).

4 Click on the Sign in button.

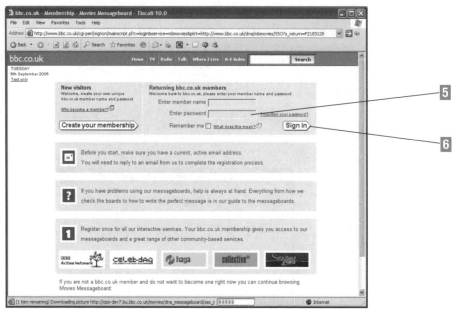

Screenshot from BBC (www.bbc.co.uk).

5 Type in your member name and password.

6 Click on the Sign In button.

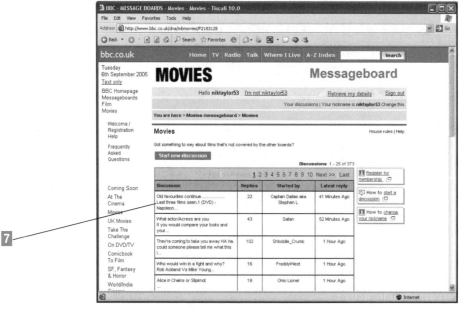

Screenshot from BBC (www.bbc.co.uk).

7 Click on the topic you would like to reply to.

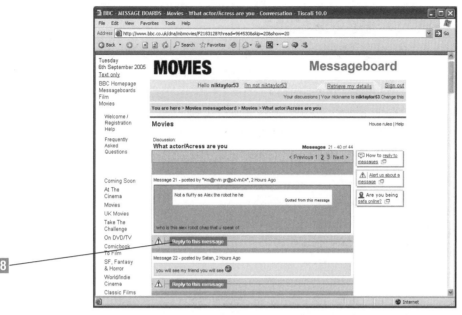

Screenshot from BBC (www.bbc.co.uk).

8 Click on the Reply to this message button for the message you would like to respond to.

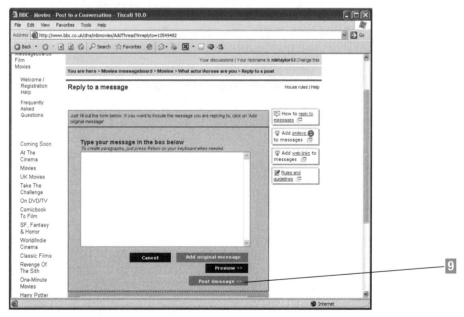

Screenshot from BBC (www.bbc.co.uk).

9 Type in your message, then click on the Post message button.

Volunteering sites

Volunteering England – www.volunteering.org.uk

Volunteer Centre Network Scotland – www.volunteerscotland.info

Volunteering Wales – www.volunteering-wales.net

Volunteer Development Agency – www.volunteering-ni.org

Charities

Charity Choice – www.charitychoice.co.uk

Charitynet – www.charitynet.org

CharityJOB – www.charityjob.co.uk

Charity People – www.charitypeople.co.uk

Newsgroups

Google Groups – http://groups.google.com

Usenet – www.usenet.com

Message boards

Yahoo! Message Boards – http://messages.yahoo.com

BBC Message Boards – www.bbc.co.uk/messageboards

IVillage Message Boards – www.ivillage.co.uk/boards

The Mail Online message boards – http://chat.dailymail.co.uk

CHAPTER 17

Business Browsing

17.1 Introduction

Any company worth its place in the *Financial Times* will now have its own website. On that website you'll find all the information you could need about a business, such as its current press releases, its contact details and so on. Listed companies will also make their finance details, such as annual reports, available for public viewing.

Such info is normally found by scrolling to the bottom of the site's home page and looking for a link such as 'About', or something similar. The link is normally tucked away out of sight so it doesn't get in the way of the main purpose of the site.

Major companies will often advertise their job vacancies on their site too. Again, any link for this sort of thing will normally be hidden away a little. Just scroll down to the bottom of the page and look for a link to 'careers', 'jobs with us' or something similar.

17.2 Getting Around Corporate Sites

The easiest way to find out information on a company is to simply head to its website. All the top businesses have some kind of online presence, and with a couple of clicks you can dig up anything from the address of the headquarters to the latest annual report.

The links that take you to this kind of information are normally tucked away near the bottom of the home page. Look for links such as 'About Us' to get to the company details.

17.2.1 Finding Information on Microsoft

1 Load the Microsoft (www.microsoft.com/uk) site in your browser.

2 Scroll down and click on the About Microsoft UK link.

3 Click on the Microsoft Press Centre link.

4 Click on the link for the details you want to find out about.

17

17.2.2

By kind permission of Microsoft (www.microsoft.com/uk).

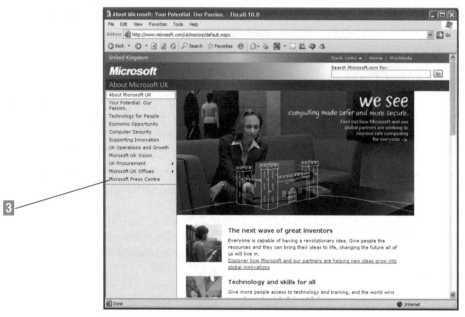

By kind permission of Microsoft (www.microsoft.com/uk).

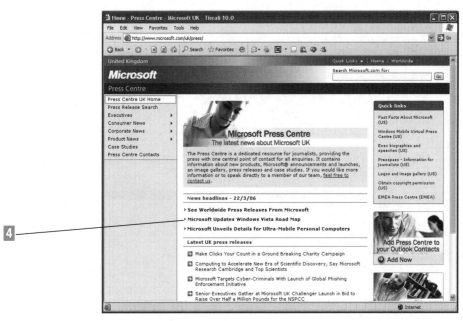

By kind permission of Microsoft (www.microsoft.com/uk).

Finding Information on Google

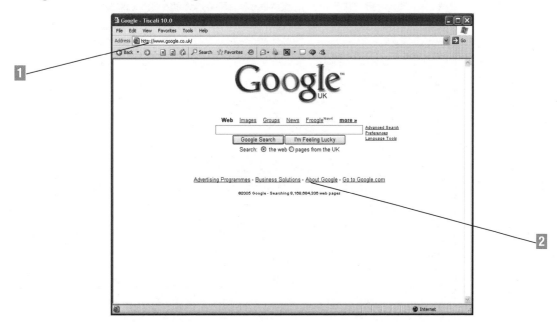

By kind permission of Google (www.google.co.uk).

1 Load the Google (www.google.co.uk) site in your browser.

2 Click on the About Google link.

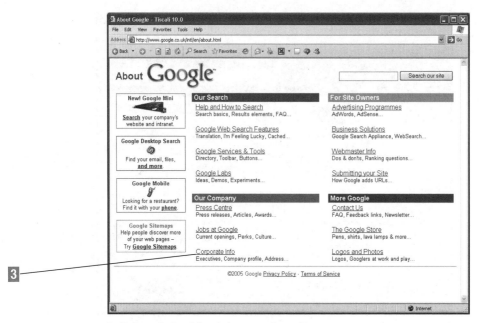

By kind permission of Google (www.google.co.uk).

3 Click on the Corporate Info link.

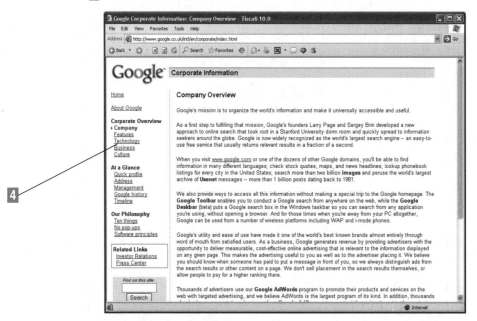

By kind permission of Google (www.google.co.uk).

4 Click on the link for the information you require.

Dealing with intranets...

Many larger companies have their own intranets. These are effectively localised versions of the Internet – they are simply made up of a network within the company.

If your company has its own intranet, it will likely be accessible through an internal website. By going onto the intranet, you will be able to access company information and services. An intranet works in a similar way to the Internet, but is not accessible via the Internet.

...or with extranets

An extranet is effectively an intranet that can be accessed from outside of its host company. The extranet can only be accessed externally by authorised users. For instance, a company may enable its customers to access the part of its intranet that shows progress of current orders.

17.3 Downloading an Annual Report

If you fancy sinking a few pennies into dabbling on the stockmarket, you'll need to do your research on the companies in which you're planning on investing. A quick way to do this is to have a nose through that firm's latest annual report. You'll find these freely available to download on the Internet and the simplest way to get one is to go to the company's website.

Look for a small link on the edges of the home page directing you to 'Investor Relations' or 'Financials'. Alternatively, you may need to click on an 'About Us' link and then follow the links to the finance pages.

17.3.1 Downloading an Annual Report from Microsoft

1　Load the Microsoft (www.microsoft.com/uk) site in your browser.

2　Click on the Investor Relations link.

3　Click on the Annual Reports link.

4　Click on the link for the report you want to see.

5　Choose the high or low bandwidth option, depending on which connection type you are using.

6　Click on the Downloads link.

7　Click on the link for the part of the report you want to download.

8　Click on the Save button on the box that appears.

9　Click on the Save in box and select a location in which you want to save the file.

10 Click on the Save button.

17

By kind permission of Microsoft (www.microsoft.com/uk).

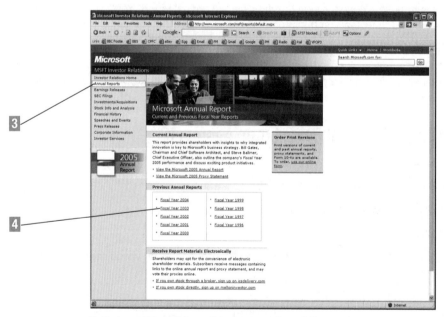

By kind permission of Microsoft (www.microsoft.com/uk).

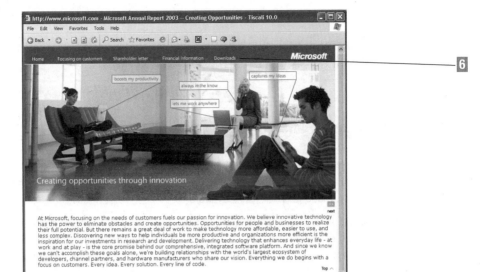

By kind permission of Microsoft (www.microsoft.com/uk).

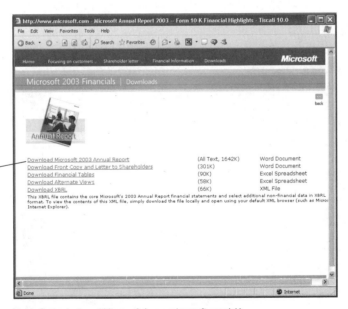

By kind permission of Microsoft (www.microsoft.com/uk).

17.4 │ Finding Corporate Jobs

Fancy a new job? Well, read through Chapter 14, where we take a look at using some of the main careers sites on the web. However, you don't have to limit yourself to job-hunting purely on these general vacancy sites.

Corporate websites normally list all their internal vacancies and may advertise positions that aren't listed elsewhere on the Net – or anywhere else for that matter. If you're keen on working for a particular firm, it's well worth taking a look at its site and making your application direct.

17.4.1 Finding a Job at Microsoft

1 Load the Microsoft (www.microsoft.com/uk) site in your browser.

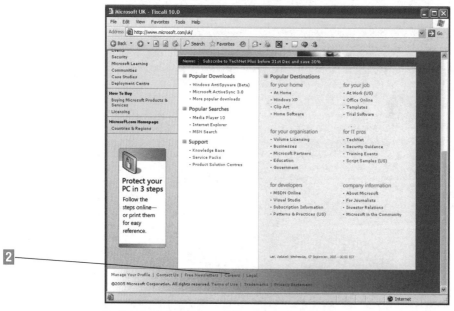

By kind permission of Microsoft (www.microsoft.com/uk).

2 Click on the Careers link at the bottom of the site.

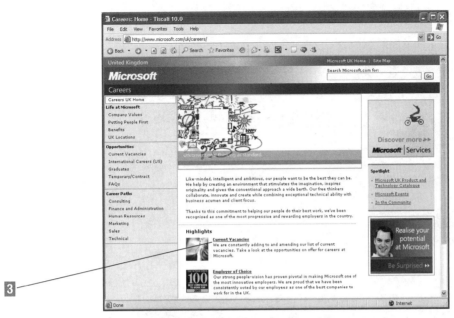

By kind permission of Microsoft (www.microsoft.com/uk).

3 Click on the Current Vacancies link.

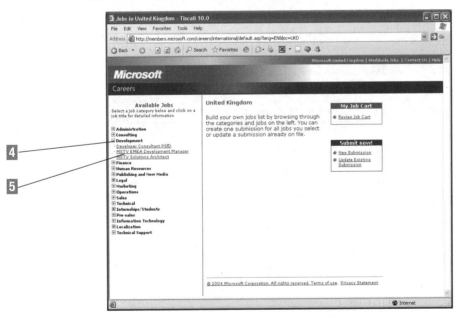

By kind permission of Microsoft (www.microsoft.com/uk).

4 Click on the category you want to check out.

5 Click on the job you're interested in.

17.4.2 Finding a Job with the BBC

1 Load the BBC (www.bbc.co.uk) site in your browser.

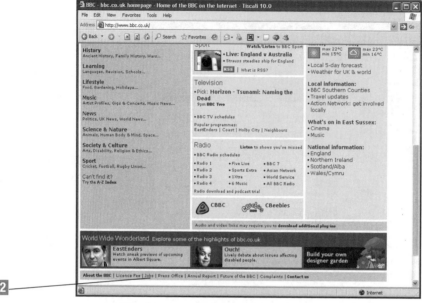

Screenshot from BBC (www.bbc.co.uk).

2 Click on the Jobs link at the bottom of the page.

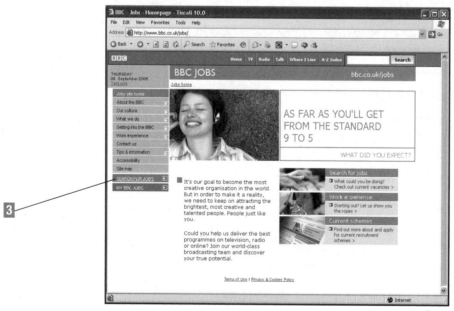

Screenshot from BBC (www.bbc.co.uk).

3 Click on the Search for jobs link.

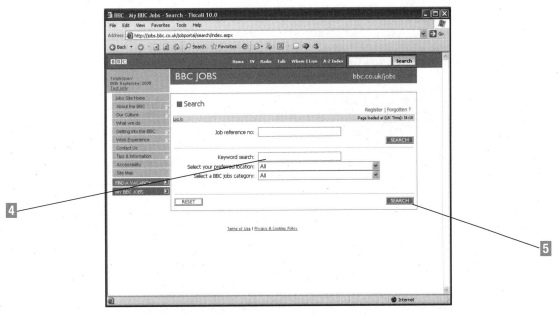

Screenshot from BBC (www.bbc.co.uk).

4 Fill in the form with the details of the job you're looking for.

5 Click on the Search button.

6 Click on the job title you're interested in.

17.4.3 Finding a Job at Barclays

1 Open the Barclays (www.barclays.co.uk) site in your browser.

2 Scroll down the page and click on the Careers link.

3 Type the job you're after into the Quick Job Search box.

4 Click on the Job Search button.

5 Click on the title of the job you're interested in.

Screenshot from Barclays (www.barclays.co.uk).

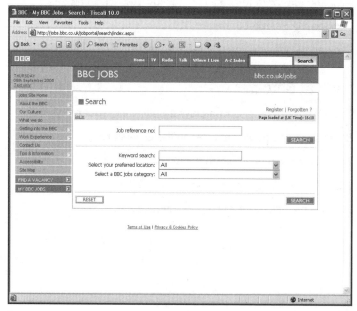

Screenshot from Barclays (www.barclays.co.uk).

Screenshot from Barclays (www.barclays.co.uk).

17.5 Handy Business Site Links

Some major companies

Microsoft – www.microsoft.com/uk

Apple – www.apple.com

Google – www.google.co.uk

Yahoo! – http://uk.yahoo.com

Barclays – www.barclays.co.uk

BT – www.bt.com

ntl – www.ntl.com

Sky – www.sky.com

Business directories

Yell – www.yell.com

Scoot – www.scoot.co.uk

Touch Local – www.touchlocal.com

Glossary

Glossary

Anti-virus	Software that protects your computer against viruses.
Attachment	A file you attach to an email.
Back button	Used in a web browser to return to the previous page viewed.
Backspace	This key on the keyboard will delete one character to the left of the cursor each time it is pressed. It is directly above the Return key, at the top right of the main keyboard. It will normally have the word Backspace written on it, but may just show a left-pointing arrow.
Base unit	Another word for your computer. This refers to the big box that contains all the electronics that make your computer work.
Bcc	See 'blind carbon copy'.
Blind carbon copy	A box you can fill in when addressing an email. When you are creating an email, you add addresses to the Bcc field if you want those people to receive the email but do not want the other recipients to see their address in the recipients list.
Boot up	Starting up your computer.
Browser	A program that enables you to view pages from the Internet.
Caps Lock	Pressing this key ensures any text you type will come out in capitals.
Carbon copy	A box you can fill in when addressing an email. When you are creating an email, you add addresses to the Cc field if those people are not the primary recipients of the message, but you want them to receive it nevertheless.
Cc	See 'carbon copy'.
Character	Any letter, number, puncutation mark, symbol or space in a written document.
Checkbox	A list of options may have checkboxes next to each. You can click on as many of these as you like to select them.

Click	Pressing the left mouse button once.
Click and drag	The process of moving an item around the screen by clicking on it with the left mouse button, then moving the mouse while the button is held down.
Click and type	Used in Microsoft Word. This mean you can double-click anywhere on the document to move the cursor to that point.
Close button	The cross button found at the top right of every window. Clicking on it closes the window you are working with.
Contact	In Outlook, a listing of an email address in your address book.
Control key	There are two Control keys at the bottom left and right of the main keyboard. Normally, they are labelled with the letters Ctrl. Holding down one of these keys along with a combination of other keys enables you to perform keyboard shortcuts.
Control Panel	One of the options you'll see when you click on the Start button. The Control Panel enables you to make changes to how your computer works.
Crash	When a computer becomes overloaded with information and stops working.
Cursor	A blinking vertical line on the screen that indicates where text will appear when you start typing.
Cursor keys	Four arrow keys found to the right of the main part of a standard keyboard. These can be used to move the cursor around the screen.
Database	This stores information which can then be searched through. For example, a company might create a database containing all of its customers' details.
Delete	This key will delete one character to the right of the cursor each time it is pressed.
Desktop	The background screen that you see when your computer has booted up.
Dialog box	A message box that appears to give you information about the program you are using. You have to click a button inside the dialog box before continuing.
Domain name	The unique name that identifies a website.
Double click	To press the left mouse button twice in rapid succession.
Download	The process of transferring data from another computer onto your own computer. Normally used to refer to transferring data from the Internet.
Drive	A device connected to your computer that is used to store data (such as your documents and other files). Most of your data will be stored on your hard drive.

Drop-down menu	A menu that appears when you click on its title, or on an arrow by the title.
Email	An electronic messaging system that enables you to instantly send a text-based message to anyone anywhere on the planet.
Encryption	Used by online shops to keep safe the credit card details entered by customers. The details are encoded so they cannot be intercepted by hackers.
Extranet	An intranet that can be accessed from outside its host company (by authorised users).
Favorites list	A list of your favourite websites, which is stored in your browser.
Field	A box on a form into which you type data.
File	A document on your computer. For instance, when you save an email on your computer, it will be stored as a file.
File format	The way a file has been saved. This determines which programs can be used to open that file.
Filename	The name given to a file on your computer. Each file stored in the same place must have a different name.
Filename extension	The three letters at the end of a filename that tell the computer what type of file it is. For instance, a file with the extension .doc will be a Microsoft Word document.
File sharer	A type of program that enables users to share files with each other. Typically used to share music and video files.
Firefox	A type of web browser.
Firewall	A type of program that prevents hackers from gaining access to your computer via the Internet.
Flag	Flags can be attached to email messages to highlight their importance.
Folder	An object used to contain files.
Form	Online, a page where you have to fill in details. For instance, if you want to buy a CD online, you have to fill in a form detailing your address and payment details.
Forward	In email, this refers to sending on a received email to another person.
Forward button	Used in a web browser to move forward by one page.
Frame	A separate section of a web page.
ftp	Stands for file transfer protocol. This is a common method for moving a file between two web sites.

Function keys	Standard keyboards have 12 function keys, labelled F1 to F12. These are found at the top of the keyboard. Each will have a different function depending on the program you are using, though some will be the same in any program. For instance, pressing F1 will always open a program's help facility.
Hacker	Someone who gains unauthorised access to computer systems.
Hard drive	A device inside your computer that is used to store data.
Help	Practically every program comes with a help feature. Opening this enables you to search for help on using the program.
History	A list of recently visited websites stored by your browser.
Home page	The page you choose to have load up automatically whenever you open your web browser.
Home page button	Used in a web browser to take you straight to your home page.
Icon	A picture on your screen that symbolises an object, such as a folder, program or file.
Inbox	The folder in your email program which stores incoming mail.
Internet	An electronic network connecting millions of computers across the world.
Internet Explorer	Example of a web browser.
Intranet	An internal network that behaves in a similar way to the Internet, but is not part of the Internet. Often used by companies to make information available to employees.
ISP	Internet service provider. This is a company which provides access to the Internet, in the same way as your phone company provides access to the telephone network.
Keyboard	Like a typewriter, but attached to your computer. This enables you to type text which then appears on the screen.
Keyboard shortcut	A combination of keys that can be pressed to quickly complete a task. For instance, you can save a document by pressing the Ctrl and S keys at the same time.
Link	Links can be text, buttons, images and so on. Clicking on a link takes you to another document (such as a web page).
Log off	The process of finishing your session on a computer without actually turning it off.
Log on	The process of typing in your name and password when you start using your computer. Logging on enables the computer to load up your personal settings.

Maximise	A button found at the top right of a window. Clicking on this makes the window fill the entire screen. If a screen is already maximised, this button will become the Restore button.
Menu	A list of tasks and commands displayed on screen. You can choose one of the commands by clicking on it.
Menu bar	Usually found near the top of a program window, this contains a number of menus. Clicking on a menu name opens that menu.
Message board	A type of website on which people can add messages for others to read.
Microsoft Office	A popular collection of programs (often known as a suite of programs). Microsoft Office contains software such as Word (for word processing), Excel (for processing calculations) and PowerPoint (for creating presentations).
Minimise	A button found at the top right of a window. Clicking on this makes the window disappear without closing it down. The window can be brought back by clicking on its button on the taskbar.
Monitor	The screen that's attached to your computer.
Mouse	A handheld device that enables you to move a pointer around on the screen. The buttons on a mouse enable you to interact with the items on the screen.
mp3	A file format that can drastically reduce the size of music files, thus making them quicker to download.
My Computer	A feature that enables you to look through all the drives and folders on your computer.
Newsgroup	A discussion group devoted to the discussion of a particular subject.
Number Lock	Found at the top left of the number pad. Pressing this key toggles Number Lock. If Number Lock is turned on, the number pad keys will type numbers when pressed.
Number pad	The numbers on the far right of a standard keyboard.
Opera	A type of web browser.
Operating system	The software that runs the computer. The most common type of operating system is Microsoft Windows.
Overtype mode	Used in word processing programs, enabling Overtype mode means any text you type will replace existing text in its path. This mode is turned on and off by pressing the Insert key.
Pane	A section of a program's window.
PC	Stands for personal computer.

Peripheral	An additional item attached to your computer. Examples of peripherals include printers, scanners and speakers.
Phishing	A scam where emails are sent out that look as though they come from a reputable organisation. The email asks for sensitive data, such as credit card details.
Pointer	A small image on the screen that moves as you move the mouse. The pointer will have a different shape depending on what you are doing.
Post	To add something to an existing web page. The term is usually used when referring to adding a comment to a message board.
Print preview	A preview of how a document will appear when it is printed.
Program	A tool that you open on your computer when you want to complete a particular task. For instance, if you wanted to type a letter, you would open a word processing program.
Quick launch toolbar	This contains shortcut buttons that open the relevant programs when clicked. This toolbar is located next to the Start button.
Radio button	A list of options may have radio buttons next to each. You can click on one of the radio buttons to select it. If you then click on another to select it, the first is deselected.
Refresh button	Used in a web browser to reload a web page.
Register	The process of becoming a member of a website. Membership normally enables you to access areas or features of the site not open to non-members.
Reply to all	An option on email programs which enables you to reply to all the recipients of an email.
Restore	A button found at the top right of a window. This is only visible if the window has been maximised. Clicking on it will return the window to its previous size.
Return	This key on the keyboard is mainly used to start a new line in a document or to accept a choice. The shape of the key is like an upside-down L. You will find it on the right-hand side of the main keyboard.
Right click	Pressing the right mouse button once.
Save	The process of storing information on your computer. When you have finished working on something, you will save it so it is still there the next time you turn on your computer.
Save as	The option used instead of Save if you want to change anything about the way in which the file is to be saved (e.g. the location in which it is stored).

Search engine	A type of website that is used to find other web pages.
Shift	This key changes what the other keys do while it is held down. For instance, if you press a letter key while holding down the Shift key and the letter, it will come out in uppercase.
Shut down	Switching off your computer.
Software	See 'program'.
Spam	Unwanted email – typically marketing scams.
Spreadsheet	A table containing text and figures, on which you can perform calculations. Spreadsheets are usually used for budgets, statistics and so on.
Start button	The button at the bottom left of the screen. Clicking on this opens all the options available to you on your computer.
Stop button	Used in a web browser to stop any more data being downloaded.
Sub-folder	A folder that is contained within another folder.
Sub-menu	A menu that is contained within another menu.
System tray	Located on the far right of the task bar, this shows the programs running in the background on your computer.
Tab	Pressing this key moves the cursor along to the next tab point. This key is located to the left of the Q key.
Taskbar	The bar that stretches along the bottom of your screen. The taskbar lists the programs currently open, as well as other information such as the time.
Title bar	The bar at the top of a window that tells you the program and file you are working with.
Toolbar	A group of buttons, normally found at the top of a program window. Each button is associated with a different command. Clicking on the button activates that command.
URL	Uniform resource locator. Simply put, this is the address you will type in to get to a specific web page.
Virus	A malicious program that spreads from computer to computer. Viruses will ofen cause damage to data stored on computers they have infected.
Web browser	See 'browser'.
Web page	A single page of information.
Website	A collection of related web pages.
Window	An enclosed area on your screen that appears when you open a program. Each program is contained within a separate window, and you can have several windows open at once.

Windows Explorer	A program that enables you to search through all the files stored on your computer.
Wizard	A program that guides you through the completion of a complicated process.
Word processor	A type of software that enables you to type letters and other documents.
World Wide Web	Often known simply as 'the web', this is a system that provides global access to all the data (such as web pages) that can be accessed by web browsers.

Index

Happy Computers ○ Happy People ○ Happy eLearning

Accompanying this book is an online course in e-Citizen from Happy eLearning, the online division of the award-winning training company Happy Computers. To register for the course, please contact:

Happy eLearning
Cityside House
Adler Street
London
E1 1EE

Website: www.happyelearning.co.uk
Email: info@learnfish.com

Tel No.: 020 7375 7300
Minicom No.: 020 7375 7349
Fax No.: 020 7375 7301

The cost of the online course is £40 (including VAT) for one licence to purchasers of this book. For those buying 100 or more licences this reduces to £12 + VAT per licence.